THE PATH
NOT TAKEN

Books by Allen Wheelis

The Path Not Taken

—

Reflections on Power and Fear
BY Allen Wheelis

—

W·W·Norton & Company

NEW YORK   *LONDON*

Printed in the United States of America.

The text of this book is composed in 11.5/14.5 Sabon,
with display type set in Bembo bold.
Composition and manufacturing by
The Maple-Vail Book Manufacturing Group.
Book design by Margaret Wagner.

First Edition

Library of Congress Cataloging-in-Publication Data

Wheelis, Allen, 1915–
The Path Not Taken : Reflections on Power and Fear /
Allen Wheelis.
p. cm.
1. Control (Psychology) 2. Fear. I. Title.
BF611.W54 1990
303.3—DC20

ISBN 0-393-02831-3

W. W. Norton & Company, Inc.,
500 Fifth Avenue, New York, N.Y. 10110
W. W. Norton & Company Ltd.,
37 Great Russell Street, London WC1B 3NU

1 2 3 4 5 6 7 8 9 0

for Mark Wheelis

Contents

10 Contents

Oh priest of signs, disquieted creature,
caught in the temple of all alphabets,
your life will soon be over.
What have you seen? What have
you feared? What have you accomplished?

—*ELIAS CANETTI*

IN THE PLAYGROUND *I crawl upon the turnabout.*
Four teenagers come racing. With one foot aboard
and one foot pushing, they strain and yell. The plat-
form revolves. Slowly. Then faster. And faster. Trees
sail before me. The boys leap off but hang on to the
bars, race with the platform. Their joyous power and
my cowering fear define the world. All of life is
stretched between these poles. The platform spins
like a top. Wind flattens my face. I hold tightly.
Faster and faster it whirls. A giant hand is pulling at
me. I cling. People running, the world blurs, twirls,
blends. Nausea. Lightness. The giant hand seizes me
roughly, is prying loose my fingers. . . .

THE PATH
NOT TAKEN

I

▬

Orbit

THE PROBLEM IS: How grasp the world? How take hold without dislodging someone else? And should we care?

I LIE ON soft earth, looking up into a clear night, into the eye of that vast spangled disk, whirling around its dark center trailing arms of frozen fire. I am looking into endless night. The spin grows faster. I am taken with vertigo. My fingers spread, I seize the grass, try to force myself back into the earth, that I not fly away. My wife, beside me, is calm.

No moon. To our right the feathery blackness of tall Douglas fir, to our left low, round trees, ghostly white. Above us a cloudless black velvet sky, sequined, glittering, minute pulses of red, green, blue, and gold; remote, icy. Beneath us the soft loam of the orchard.

"I feel the earth," she says, "its tremendous size and

weight, the slow turning . . . and, sometimes, I think I can feel the even slower movement around the sun. "

Why is it, I wonder, that she is part of the world, while I stand outside trying to grasp the world? Perhaps because she trusts it and I don't. I try to stop the turning, she goes with it.

A mild night. Windless. The trees are still.

"Once," she says, "I thought that if I exercised my eyes, if I practiced hard, I could make them very strong. Then I would be able to see a great distance . . . maybe a mile. . . . How far can one see?"

"As far as light can travel," I say.

"Farther," she says. She raises an arm, points. "See that black space? Sight sinks in there . . . goes on forever."

A faint breeze moves across our faces. Apple blossoms fall, alight like snowflakes in her dark hair. *Like snowflakes:* With words I try to grasp the world.

"The world has become very large," she says.

"Oh, look!" she cries, then points. I see nothing but night sky, stars. "It's moving. . . . There! Bright. . . . Must still be sunlight up there." I look harder, see nothing. "It grows faint, then bright. See! Now faint . . . now bright. It moves. . . . It's tumbling . . . slowly . . . over and over . . . like a barrel."

She sees better than I, and farther. I aim my gaze along her upstretched arm, and presently among the fixed stars make out the star that moves.

THAT WAS SPUTNIK. A great leap in power. The world stood in awe, jaws agape, squinting heavenward for a glimpse, some faint metallic glint, of the tiny moon we had hurled into the sky, becoming thereby meddlers in the celestial mechanics of which previously we had been but observers. Newspapers carried a diagram to explain this latest marvel: a tower projecting from a spherical earth, a man atop the tower throwing a rock which falls in a steep curve, returning to earth a short distance away. A more sophisticated but still Stone Age man with a slingshot throws his rock farther, the arc of fall more gradual; at Crécy a longbowman achieves a much greater reach; gunpowder hurls a projectile thirty miles; and now rocketry imparts such a thrust that the force that would have our missile fly away into the void equals the pull of the earth that would bring it down. Equipoised between these forces, it hangs there like the moon, circling over us, effortlessly, forever—as the earth moves around the sun, as the sun circles the dark eye of the galaxy, as the galaxy itself spirals perhaps about some primal and final black hole.

NOTHING STAYS. Presently, being able, we throw our rock even harder. It moves in a widening orbit, drifts away.

We too are drifting away. We struggle to hold the world in our grasp, but without our knowing we fall away. What is this world we're always wanting, always trying to grasp, always losing?

In the beginning the world is the womb. We are fully and tightly enclosed, tied by a gnarled rope. There follows that most violent expulsion, shock and terror, slash of cord, and the world is lost. And found again. The

world is the breast. Bleeding cord is consoled at flowing nipple; we latch on with mouth, dig in with fingers.
Presently the world enlarges, includes now a face bending over, a smile, a lullaby, the sound of footsteps. The
world is mother. The fingers relax; the world slips away
a bit, becomes larger.

The world now is father, brother, sister, aunt, por-
ridge, orange juice, bowel movement; the world becomes
family, home, Christmas tree; becomes school and
bicycle and skiing, and a girl with dark hair and smil-
ing eyes; becomes ambition, visions of the future, children of our own; becomes automobiles, airplanes, trips
to distant countries, history, world affairs, the threat
of war. The world slips away, we're falling outward,
but the view becomes ever more grand. Shining and
bright, like a blue jewel, the world spins there before
us, seemingly within our grasp, while we, like a satellite
weather station in widening orbit, camera pointed
steadily earthward, see the world with increasing com-
prehension, but remain unaware of the void behind us
into which we are falling.

THE GREATEST ENLARGEMENT of world takes place
in adolescence. Centrifugal force increases, we are hurled
away. The family that had been so large a part of our
world, indeed all of the foreground, recedes, shrinks,
all but disappears. We fall back, fall away. The world
is vast, enlarging, while we are shrinking, our life
diminishing. "We are a phantom flare of grieved desire,"
wrote Thomas Wolfe, "a ghostling and phosphoric

flicker of immortal time." In my teens, in the thirties, finding myself so small a part of something suddenly so vast, this abruptly deepened perspective on the world found its definition, its most perfect expression, in the novels of Wolfe, in those trains of his hurtling through the night across those vast plains.

As this world view took shape, I felt myself entering upon maturity, coming to grips with the world, approaching something like mastery—like Gide in his garret, late at night, pen poised above paper, looking out over the snow-covered roofs of a sleeping Paris, saying, "Now you and I will come to terms." I didn't know that I had fallen *away* from the world, that this new and exciting view was a function of greater distance, relative to a continuing fall, hence no more final than those it had replaced. It seemed, rather, that in the past I had seen the world through the colored glass of a child but that now, having reached a stable orbit, I saw it as it is, the way things are, the real thing, and that this view, therefore, though it would be further clarified and refined, need never be superseded.

YEARS PASS, years of unnoticed fall, and one day, in the fifties, reading Salinger, or perhaps the early stories of Updike, I begin thinking of Wolfe and realize I haven't heard much about him in recent years, and I look back at the page before me and realize suddenly that the world has changed, that that vision which had seemed so final has been replaced. A different world is portrayed here, different not in the sense that individual differences of

style and temperament make for unique vision—the
works of Hemingway, Wolfe, and Faulkner being
instantly distinguishable one from another—but different in the sense that the world addressed in common,
although in their several distinctive ways, by Hemingway, Wolfe, and Faulkner, is most certainly not the
world of Henry James and, likewise, is not the world
of Salinger and Updike.

NOW it is the eighties and Salinger is gone, and Updike
a senior citizen, and one day, reading Rezzori or Kun-
dera or Gombrowicz, I find once again that the world
has changed.

I'm falling, falling, and the farther I fall the faster,
and it's long been clear that no view is final, that all of
us are falling, that senses fail, vision dims, sound is
muffled, and all that is left of that too solid earth and
its cloud-capped towers is that ephemeral blue dream
reeling away in the void.

II
—
World

HOW TO LIVE? How grasp the world? Race with the strong, cower with the weak?

THE WORLD CHANGES under our hands; we are flung here, immersed, struggling, floundering toward elusive goals. From gladness to despair is but a moment. Light darkens. Never can we lift our heads above the surface of the world to look about and see how things really are. Indeed, how things *really* are is being determined by how *we* are behaving, is always changing; and each of us is shaping that objective world in which we live, which we can never know.

I AM SEVEN YEARS OLD; the other boys range up to thirteen. We are playing baseball on stony ground near my house. I am at shortstop. A hard-hitter sends the ball flashing toward me; I put out a glove, but flinch; the ball strikes a stone, whizzes by. I am running ashamedly after it when I hear my father call my name. A harsh, stentorian summons. I go to the house, stand below the window of his sickroom. "I will not permit a son of mine to be a coward!" The voice throbs with fury, with contempt, outrage. "When a ball comes at you like that, you *stand in the way.* If you can't catch it in your glove, you *stop it with your body!* Now you get back out there and don't you ever let me see you do that again!"

SUCH EXPERIENCES, of which there were many, taught me that at the very center of me was something craven. A softness that made the knees weak. A maternal protectiveness of self, instead of daring and disregard. The stuff of which I was made was fear; the right stuff was bravery. Life became a project of denying what I was while trying to become something I was not. The real me must not be seen.

The movie *High Noon* portrays the stripping away of all those social supports which may conceal the core. No one will stand by the targeted sheriff; as the killers arrive, he is absolutely alone—abandoned by wife, by friends, by deputies, by church, by community. The drama depends upon that abandonment, upon a situation having come about in which the usually concealed essence of a man will unavoidably be exposed. The soul of the sheriff proves to be unflinching courage, and I unhesitatingly extended that finding to the actor Gary Cooper, and to all other men whom I admired, while knowing in my heart that, however I might try, it would never be true of me.

I AM NINE YEARS OLD and am bullied by the other boys. As we stream out of school, they tug at my clothes, trip me; one confronts me in unexpected friendliness as another kneels unnoticed behind me. A bad time. Always toppled backwards.

One day I encounter Roy, my archtormentor, on a deserted road. He drops a loop of rope over my head. "Nice tie," he says, takes the short end and yanks as, with his other hand, he forces the knot into my throat. We scuffle. He slaps me. I push, he falls. When he gets up, he has become serious: I have been aggressive, that's what he wanted; I have given him license; now he need not hold back. I see in his face a surging zeal. I flail and retreat; he moves in. Unexpectedly I land a blow that interferes with his breathing, and immediately press my advantage, hit him in the face. He throws up his left arm, I hit him in the ear.

I am moving forward. Now *I* feel the fierce joy. What my father has done to me, I can do to another. I land my fist in his midriff; he reels back. A different expression comes to his eyes. Fear, that despicable thing, that craveness uniquely my own—it has leapt from me to him. There it is, *mine,* in his eyes. And with that leap we are transformed: I now am the brave one, he the coward. I push him back. He twists away, I deliver a rain of blows.

And now I encounter in myself something new,

something other than bravery: I have *become* my father, I am going to crush him. I feel deep joy. I grab him by the shirt, jerk him toward me; he sees my fist coming at his eye; his face crumples. I hesitate. Predator with partially mangled prey, what shall I do? He has been tormenting me: Why not take revenge? Delight in it? He begins to cry.

The paths diverge. I look both ways. I see myself more truly in Roy's fear than in my father's harshness. I let him go.

I did not fight again. Often with longing and with loss I remembered the fierce delight, the exultant moving in for the kill. I went the other way, found my place and my work among those who are afraid. I understand them better. I help them be less afraid. I cannot help myself.

MY FATHER entered into me. Day by day, insidiously, he usurped inner ground that should by rights be mine. There now is his voice, his fury, his judgment. What he demands is that I demand nothing. Meekness and self-abnegation are the price of his tolerance. If I regard myself as nothing, he will leave me alone, but should I get any fancy ideas, he will slap me down. To exist, I must abjure power.

THE WORLD is full of danger and opportunity. The strong adapt by changing the world, the weak by changing themselves. The weak look inward at desires, outward at possibilities of gratification, measure the danger, find the risk to be high, and try to bring things in line by reducing their needs. The unafraid leap into the fray, seize such power as they can, move things around, rearrange the world to fit their needs.

I AM SEVENTEEN. The woman I love, ten years older, has told me never again to call her. I wander the streets of Baton Rouge. A drizzle of rain, the air motionless and chill. A day of vast silence, the drip of water, and, far in the distance, the disappearing sound of a car. Visions of violent acts, of tuberculosis, suicide notes.

I walk along a wall of gray brick topped in wisteria. Heavy purple blossoms hang beside my face. I stop before an iron gate, look into a garden of oleander, gardenias, roses. The heavy scents pour forth. Sinuous vertical bars rise above me to a filigree arch of vines, leaves, grapes. I grasp the bars, think: I will remember this moment. However long I live. Pain is branding it into my soul: the chill of wet iron, the flaking green paint, the whisper of rain, numb feet in wet shoes, the drip, drip, drip. My knuckles become white, my arms rigid. The pain swells, moves toward a more ample expression, perhaps a throwing back of my head and sobbing, perhaps a shaking of the gate till someone appears to love me, to drive me away, or to call the police.

Then there comes to me a thought, fully formed, coming not from the center of the pain but from a place slightly apart: *It is not necessary to suffer like this.* I stand still, startled, pursue the thought: I must be doing this to myself. The pain is given, but I am *choosing* to hallow it, to drive it toward some dark fruition, to walk for hours through a wet city, staring into forbidden gardens.

This is an order of power not much needed if one can bend the world to one's wants. When Nero is bored, he is not thrown back on inner resources; he tosses Christians to the lions. But if one is powerless in the world, power over one's self is a matter of life and death.

WORKS of imaginative reach bear a reciprocal relation to the lives of their creators. They portray, and in fantasy realize, things lacking and longed for and only potential in the creator's life. What the artist aspires to but can never achieve in living becomes that which exerts the most lasting and powerful effect on his imagination, becoming thereby the subject of his work, his task.

WHO but a weakling would analyze power?

IN THIS WORK, glancing back at the path taken, I examine the path not taken.

III
—

The Will to Power

THE WILL to power is that quality of a living thing that leads it to grab hold of its environment, to take in what nourishes it, as much as it can, to shoulder aside whoever is interested in the same thing, to trample whatever stands in its way, to grow, to become big and strong, and to multiply. There is no moderation; nothing is too much. The aim of the maggot is to make more maggots, to transform the entire universe into maggots. The drive is blind, knows no internal limit, will continue until stopped.

FOR MOST of the duration of life on earth the principal form of power was physical—the ability to rend, to tear, to seize, to pin down, to destroy, to gobble up. For mankind such abilities have become less important. Significant power in human affairs is now in the

form of money, property, position, acclaim, posses-
sions, influence, love.

The guises of power are so various, so dissembled
that power ceases to be recognized as such. We would
have it that human life is discontinuous with life in the
tide pools, in the jungle, that mind or spirit, something
far removed from power, has come to be the essence of
human life. We delude ourselves. The holders of great
power may be physically frail, gentle in manner, tender
in sentiment, Christian by profession, may wear but a
loincloth; but power is power, and its nature is to grab
hold, to seize possession, to overwhelm. Whatever
appears in human life that seems unrelated to power,
or even—like love, like charity, like self-sacrifice—contrary to it, is, if it endures, but another mask of power.

OBSERVE the single cell. It moves about, this way and
that, exploring, seeking. What does it want? It wants
to seize the nutrient environment, take it in, grow big-
ger, stronger. It has heard God's voice: Be fruitful and
multiply.

IT COMES ABOUT in time that a group of cells associate themselves into a community. Something new. Are
not these several cells hampered in their competition
by virtue of, as it were, holding hands? Why, yes, very
likely. And whenever so hampered, they perish. But it
comes about eventually that some such association is
not hampered but advantaged, finds itself the possessor

of superior strength, greater than the summation of its constituent strengths, whereupon the association endures. The will to power of the individual cell is surrendered to the whole. The will of the individual cell comes to be not power but cooperation, faithful service in its subordinate place and function in the life of the organism.

A THOUGHT EXPERIMENT.

I am alone in the world. I have always been alone. Nothing and no one to protect me. Just my wits and my strength and such weapons as I find or contrive. In the driving wind the freezing rain is like arrows.

I find a cave—a cave, I discover, that has been found already by a bear. I will drive him out if I can. I do not think: This is not fair, it belongs to him. I do not wonder: Who has the greater need, he or I? I drive him out.

I am hungry; a fawn comes within range of my stone. I do not ponder contending rights, do not weigh the fawn's life against my own; I kill.

I am warm; I am full, the day is over, I lie down to sleep. I keep my club close to hand.

One day I encounter another man. I cannot read his gestures or understand his strange sounds. I give him a wide berth, go my own way. He follows. I make threatening gestures, he retreats. At night I do not sleep well. How close is he? What does he intend? The next day, at my bidding, he comes closer. I kill him.

For the solitary savage there is no guilt, no right and no wrong.

Years pass. Millennia. Now I live in a community. There are ten or twenty of us. We hunt together, sit around the fire together, are frightened as one by the evil spirits of the forest. Within this group I do not kill, do not steal, do not deceive. I am no longer sovereign, I live within limits, I have become moral.

Another group moves into our territory. They are fishing in our streams, killing our game. One of our men is found with an arrow in his back. We lament, we wail, we rage. Our chief calls a council. We are endangered, he tells us; our way of life is threatened; we must avenge our loss. We beat our drums to drive away our fear, paint horizontal stripes of red and white on our bodies. At midnight we set forth. In silence and stealth we approach the sleeping camp. We drink strong beer. Two boys with torches set fire to the straw huts. As the occupants rush out, silhouetted by the flames, we let loose our arrows, our spears. When our enemies are in blind panic, we fall upon them, club them to death. Some of the women we rape; we throw the babies into the fire; we kill everybody, burn everything. On the march home we are content, relaxed, fulfilled. We sing, we laugh, we are triumphant.

Sovereignty has passed to the group. For the group there is no good and no evil.

I V

Collectives

WHAT BINDS us together in a community is shared beliefs. Vital yet unnoticed, like the air we breathe, they constitute the meaning of life, tell us how to interpret our experience, determine *what* we experience. With them we grasp the world, make sense of what happens to us, find our place, arrange our lives into known patterns. We feel at home; we know how to live.

But something is left over. Something of bereavement or pain or mystery is unaccounted for, experience of which we cannot make sense, with which we cannot come to terms. This is the margin of terror. If we are loyal to the received wisdom, we look away, pretend it does not exist, is of no importance, a deviation, a neurosis perhaps; experience is falsified, but shared beliefs are not impugned. The received wisdom spreads its sheltering umbrella.

If one is loyal to deviant experience, one is apostate

to the common faith and hence estranged from those who live by it, which is pretty much everybody. One finds oneself alone in a desert where one's specialness is scant comfort.

NOTHING STAYS. The world would fling us away, spins like a carousel. The received interpretations no longer work, don't fit, don't take hold. We cannot grasp the world.

Some people don't hear the screaming; the old fictions still work. Some hear it keenly: The chalk has worn down, the fingernail drags across an endless blackboard, the sky is empty.

IN TIMES OF PEACE most people find it possible to believe, at least nominally, in the received wisdom. In times of great social upheaval—the Napoleonic Wars, the Russian Revolution—the received wisdom is shattered for everyone. The world is lost—because it was these shared beliefs, now overturned and discredited, that constituted the world.

THE HOLIEST FICTIONS designate what is right and what is wrong, constitute a scheme of things that redeems the way things are. The way things are is the will to power of groups. The scheme of things conceals the ways of power behind a lofty and glittering façade. The whole system hangs on the power of images and words, the keeping of promises, the observance of convention.

The reign of order, Valéry writes, which is that of symbols and signs, always results in fairly general disarmament, "beginning with visible arms and gradually spreading to the will. Swords get thinner and vanish, characters get rounder. The age when fact was dominant fades imperceptibly away. Under the names *foresight* and *tradition,* the future and the past, which are imaginary perspectives, dominate and restrain the present."

We must note, however, as Valéry does not, that the general disarmament is only *within* the system of order. The brutality and barbarism of the individual have but passed to the collective. The sword of the citizen gets thinner, vanishes; the sword of the state gets longer, sharper.

CELLS SERVE the organism. The organism grows larger and more powerful by virtue of finding the best way to exploit its constituents. Slaves may be made to man the oars and drive the galley, but it requires the constant attention of a slavemaster cracking the whip. But if the slaves can be converted to a faith in the ship and its mission, then no slavemaster will be needed—he will now be free to help with the cannon—while the ship slices forward ever faster, with more power, more dangerous to its enemies.

THERE is no alternative to power, no other position—not Christianity nor the Golden Rule nor brotherly love nor nonviolence; not self-sacrifice nor the turning of the other cheek. For all these various abnegations of power by parts of a whole are, unwittingly, in the service of increased power to the whole; and the morality created by such renunciations is used by the aggregate to increase the power with which it then pursues more power.

GOOD AND EVIL come into existence as defined by power, and are shaped to protect power. They filter down from rulers, magistrates, educators, from bishops, priests, and Sunday school teachers to parents, who shape the conscience of children, imprint the limits, instill the guilt.

Order and safety are maintained; citizens need not bear arms; violence is proscribed, banished beyond borders. And so it comes about that the modern state is thought to be a moral state, even a Christian state, the source and the defender of morality, of civilization, of high culture. But the morality that is here rightly ascribed to the state is *internal,* the lawfulness of cells within an organism. In its conduct with other states, and with those barbarians beyond its borders, the state is a killer. And utterly self-righteous in its exterminations. The state claiming morality is like a murderer claiming innocence by pointing out that the constituent parts of his body behaved lawfully during the performance of the crime.

The state does not intend *itself* to become moral; it requires morality of its subjects as the necessary basis of its own amoral power, of its continued ability to conduct international brigandage abroad and the torture of political prisoners at home.

The unselfishness of individuals empowers the selfishness of states. The selflessness of patriots becomes the arrogance of nations. Morality constricts and diminishes the life of the individual as it strengthens and enlarges the life of the collective.

V

Love

SO . . . How grasp the world?

NO THING lends itself to seizure. We shall grasp nothing without force. Whatever we desire—money, sex, beauty, land, love, honor, fame—power is the means, the only hope for our uncertain endeavors.

We are nailed to it as to an iron cross. We long for some respite short of death, we make tender arrangements; but love, caring, ecstasy, moments of melting closeness are still power relations. We never lay down our weapons.

Romantic love expresses our yearning to be unarmed, to come together with that magical other who is shaped to us as form to cast, the absolute reciprocal. With her, contest will be precluded, she and I will fuse into one indivisible whole. We long for such, we yearn, we dream of total surrender, of a love death, an ecstasy that will lift us above and beyond our armed state. Yet always the drawn sword lies between the sleeping Tristan and Iseult.

And finding that submission is not possible for us, we hope cravenly it may yet be possible for her, that she will surrender, will say, "I am thine, do with me as you will, I cannot resist you."

And maybe she will. For a moment, perhaps, but no longer. She may wish it, she may mean it, may speak in utter belief, but is no more able than you to abjure power. There is no love so exalted as to exclude it. It insinuates itself into the deepest affinity. When the spent bodies fall apart, there it is again, a drawn sword between them.

AND NO END TO IT. Over and over, the entwining and coursing of bodies, the taking her, having her, knowing her. And it may be fun for her, too; she may even want it—though not with his urgency. A drive for him, for her something more elective. Her priorities lie elsewhere. Thus it comes about that sex is something that women have and that men want. A trade must be arranged: She allows the conquest which potentiates his sexuality, and in exchange exacts from him her own version of power—support, recognition, protection, commitment.

I AM CROUCHING in a low space. The light is dim. The far reaches of this vast room are in darkness. All around me are the pushed-aside but not yet discarded

accumulations of my past. A bookcase of cleaning supplies, coffee filters, paper towels; a heap of luggage,
duffel bags, overnight cases; a Danish chair of leather
and gray tweed, one leg loose; Joan's loom from the
sixth grade—the bit of fabric on the warp, frozen by
the passing of childhood, has not grown in thirty years.
A case of whiskey, wooden shutters, tables, bed-
springs, toys, books, manuscripts, boxes of old checks,
business records, office supplies, rugs with crumbling
rubber pads. Gear belonging to Joan's former boy-
friends, now scattered and replaced: scuba equipment,
fins, goggles, a projection machine, a power saw. Slides,
photographs, puppets, Christmas ornaments, dolls. The
light is dim because these things are piled so high they
block the illumination from the two light bulbs.

From concrete floor to rough plaster ceiling is five
feet; I walk deeply bent over. My back hurts. The house
towers above me. My life presses down on me, bends
me forward and down like a bow.

I can never sort through all this junk. Should call
someone to get it, cart it all away. Don't look. Just let
it go. Start over, with an empty room. At my age? I
spot a box which, I remember, contains three chess sets,
two of ivory, one of alabaster. Valuable things here. In
a pile of rugs I recognize the fringe of an antique Isfa-
han which lay on the floor of my office for twenty years.
The funeral urn design, blues and greens and violets,
reds and rusts, and beside each urn the phoenix. Life
springs from ashes, it's true, but new life; the old does
not spring, does not return. My life is bound to this
place, to this body, to memories that will go with me
as unavoidably as fillings in my teeth.

Footsteps above. Light, quick. Footsteps of utter femaleness.

The far wall of this dim space—I can just make it out—is curved. I see the impressions of the wood frame in which the concrete was poured a hundred years ago. Directly above me is the dining room. Circular. White fabric walls with elaborate delicate moldings, three pairs of high French doors opening onto a garden. Azaleas, wisteria, bougainvillaea, camelias, rhododendrons. Above each set of doors a half circle of glass, mullions radiating as in a spread fan. High ceiling. In that room we sit to eat together. For all these years. On the day we bought this house, forty years ago, she brought a bottle of champagne. We sat on the floor of that room and drank to each other, to the future. I still can smell the dust, the paint. How I loved it! The quality of light, the emptiness around us that was to fill up with our lives.

Directly above the dining room is our bedroom. Again the curved wall, casement windows opening over a park. Cypress, pine, blue spruce, purple plum. At night we lie on the large bed, windows open, curtains stirring slightly in the warm breeze, dim reflected light, moving leaves and branches on the white ceiling. Bodies press together, strain for oneness, achieve it for a moment, fuse, hold it, fall reluctantly, exhaustedly, back into separateness.

Above the bedroom, accessible only by a vertical ladder affixed to the wall of a closet—a closet so stuffed with old clothes, boxes, vacuum cleaners, suitcases that merely to open the door is to risk being knocked down, accessible therefore only to me—above the bedroom is the roof, the summit. The world, glittering with sun and color, opens up, lies at one's feet: bay, bridge, the Presidio, ocean liners, the Transamerica pyramid, the towering monoliths of downtown San Francisco.

This house, this living, breathing organism, holding all the markings and detritus of our lives, holding her of those quick steps and holding me, and all our past, towers up vertically over me. I am in its nethermost depths.

We call this place the dungeon to distinguish it from the storeroom which adjoins it, which has a seven-foot ceiling. "Where did you put it?" my wife will ask. "In the storeroom?" "No, the storeroom is full; I put it in the dungeon." "I'll never be able to find it," she will say. And indeed, she will not. Nor, probably, will I. Since the dungeon is so difficult to enter and so hard to move about in, she seldom comes here. The things stored here are heavy, and it is I who bring them. Once here they seldom leave. I lose track of what is here and where.

The disorder of this place does not reflect me; I am known to be exceedingly neat. This requires explanation. I am like one of those stars that undergo erratic motion explicable only by the supposition that they are twinned with nonvisible stars the masses of which account for the observed perturbations. This mess around me is my perturbation. It is she of those footsteps with whom I am twinned. Her mass leads me to behave uncharacteristically.

For she trusts things, believes that beautiful things cannot but enrich our lives, while I distrust things, know that beautiful or not, they bring disorder, entropy, and death. So it has come about over the years that she would bring things into this house and I would throw things out. She would bring fabrics, furniture, pictures, wall hangings, musical instruments, books, phonograph records, photographs, china, vases, linens, lamps, cooking utensils, gadgets, games. And soon the blessed emptiness of our new house was lost. To preserve order, I would give things away, constantly, and the basement stayed neat. But eventually I realized that this task was endless, that I could never rest, that she would bring in new things quite as fast as I could get rid of old things, that I was doomed, therefore, to stand forever in the cellar of our lives with a shovel, trying to keep up with the avalanche coming down from above. A time came when I rebelled. I would shovel no more. Let the stuff accumulate. Maybe eventually the backup, the back pressure, would neutralize her acquisitiveness—as the production of new automobiles might someday conceivably be halted at the factory by virtue of the highway to the city becoming so clogged with cars that there was no place for new cars to go, no room for them even to roll off the assembly line.

"Isn't that the most wonderful chair?" she says; we are in a store of Scandinavian furniture. "Look at the curve of the arms. Like the wings of a bird. It would be just perfect in our living room—where the blue chair is now. That blue chair is getting shabby anyway. We should replace it." "Where will we put it?" I ask. "Maybe in Joan's room." "There's no space left in Joan's room." "Well . . . the dungeon then." "There's no space left in the dungeon," I tell her. "Well . . . we will just

have to give some things away . . . to make some space."
"Very well," I say in my vast and patient deviousness,
"but don't buy this new chair until you have first done
that giving away of some things in the dungeon so there
will be a place to put the blue chair, so that this new
bird chair can go in the living room." Sadly she
acquiesces, we pass on through the store. And once
home, of course, she forgets about looking in the dungeon, has no time and no interest for sorting through
and disposing of this mess.

VI
—

Sovereignty

MORAL INDIVIDUALS are those who have been persuaded, insidiously, unknowingly, that self-interest is
best served by a certain regard for others. The collective insists on it, it is taught from the cradle, it becomes
second nature, indistinguishable from first nature, a
given and reliable guide to right conduct; one has only
to listen to the still inner voice. The antecedents of conscience are forgotten.

FEAR, as well as morality, opposes the individual will
to power. And often it is unclear whether it is morality
that sets the limit, or fear masquerading as morality.
Fear issues into inhibition and passivity, seedbed of envy.

BECAUSE we are afraid, we live in groups, packs,
hordes, crowds. The antelope in the herd has a better

chance of escaping the lion. Alone one is weak; in the crowd one will become strong. If the crowd grows rapidly and achieves great density, a moment of discharge will arrive, leveling hierarchies of power, making all equal; there will be no one above giving orders, making us feel weak and afraid, because everything above will be destroyed; we will surge through the streets, smashing windows and doors, overturning police cars, burning palaces. Even pacific crowds, in theaters, at rock concerts, stadiums, achieve their moments of discharge, of symbolic destruction and leveling, in the roar of applause, the packed and swaying bodies, the stamping feet.

The very strong and daring move toward the group, not in fear but to seize control, to command its power, to lead. The very weak avoid the group lest they be trampled. And then there are those who cannot or will not adjust, whom the group discards. Alone they hear from far away the roar of the crowd, and in their isolation feel even weaker, more desolate, yearn bleakly for that loss of boundaries, that oneness with something huge and powerful.

WHEN MEN LIVE each on his own, morality does not exist. Such men have freedom without limit, but the enjoyment of that freedom is slight; for each must be on guard against all others, and each must scrounge alone for food and shelter.

It appears advantageous for all, therefore, if each surrenders a bit of freedom in exchange for group solidarity. So each gives up his right to murder, to steal, to deceive. Now all are less free but more safe. Without fear they live together, secure against predators, hunt more successfully in a group, build better shelters.

The rights that were surrendered are not lost, but passed upward. The group comes into being by collecting the surrendered rights of its constituent individuals. The group itself surrenders nothing, is subject to no rule, is free to use its aggregate force for such acts of murder, of stealing, of deceiving, as it may see fit. And it does often so see fit. The members of the group have become moral; the group is now the predator. The restraints consequent to surrendered individual freedoms constitute the stuff of morality.

The aggregate power of the surrendered rights is exercised not by all acting in concert but by rulers. We hope that the freedoms we have surrendered will be exercised by our rulers for the benefit of all. Such is rarely the case.

THE RELATIONSHIP of the individual to the state is not that of cell to multicellular organism. For the cell surrenders *all* autonomy to the organism, whereas the individual person withholds some initiative from the state. The state, in its will to power, would have it that individuals become like cells; and occasionally, when the state is exceedingly powerful, it may bring this about. The autonomy we retain as individuals constitutes a limit to the degree to which the state may command our compliance.

The extent to which the individual is committed to the shared beliefs of his community measures the extent to which he has been willing to give up individual power in the interest of community. When shared beliefs are firm, the collective wields great power, its constituents correspondingly less. When shared beliefs are destroyed, the collective loses power.

AT THE TOP of the hierarchy of social organization is the realm of sovereignty, where there are no rules. Here the hypocrisy is extreme; for the stability and solidarity of the collective are dependent upon the confidence of its constituent subordinate collectives and individuals that the government is itself bound by those principles which protect its constituents, as well as its neighbors, from the abuse of its power. So the spokesmen for the sovereign amoral nation are constantly proclaiming the nation's morality, its commitment to justice, freedom, and peace, whereas in fact, they are leading the nation in the pursuit of more power by whatever means promise success. Insofar as this pursuit is curbed at all, it is curbed by fear of retaliation by other sovereign states and fear of insurrection at home.

The proclaiming of morality by the state is so loud and so constant, becomes such a litany that the leaders of a nation may hypnotize themselves, may come to believe their own public relations act. Concurrent with careful plotting for the annexation of the Philippine Islands, the American government advanced the fiction that the unpredictable fortunes of war were making America the unwilling and reluctant recipient and custodian of the islands. And when, later, the deed having been done, a group of clergymen called upon President McKinley, he explained just how he had arrived at his decision: "I walked the floor of the White House night after night until midnight; and I am not ashamed to tell you gentlemen that I went on my knees and prayed to Almighty God for light and guidance more than one night. And one night it came to me this way—that there was nothing left for us to do but to take them all, and to educate the Filipinos, and uplift and civilize and Christianize them. And by God's grace do the very best we could by them, as our fellowmen for whom Christ also died. And then I went to bed and went to sleep and slept soundly."

MORALITY is not a vision of ends, however desirable, but a system of restraints in the pursuit of any end. States speak the language of morality without the intention of being limited by it. They behave as they see fit, and the way they see fit is then declared to be moral. If they embark on conquest, it is in "self-defense." If they invade and take over a neighboring state, it is at the "invitation" of that state to maintain order, liberty, justice, etc. Since there is no tribunal with the authority to disallow such claims, the state has the last word. And its last word is always a pious assertion of morality.

WHEN WE CONDEMN, as we often do, the action of a sovereign entity as wrong, for the torture of political prisoners, for example, we do so on the basis of an individual morality that obtains *within* the collective. We extend those limits, rules, and restraints, and demand that the state itself observe them.

And how does the challenged state respond? It says: "Like all civilized nations, we absolutely condemn the torture of political prisoners. Be assured it does not happen here." When presented with names, dates, photographs: "These regrettable incidents were the unauthorized actions of certain guards, who will be apprehended and punished." When it is demonstrated that the practice continues: "We do it only when absolutely necessary for national security." When pressed further: "Other nations do it, too, including your own." And finally: "Your visa is canceled. Go home."

So what then does it mean when we condemn a state for evil acts? It means that we believe there *should* be limits, rules, to which the state voluntarily restricts itself, however lofty the ends in view which might call for their suspension, and that if it does not, it should be forcibly restrained and punished. Which is to say, there *should* be a morality of sovereign states. And so perhaps there should. But there *is* not. And should ever it come about, the states it restrained would no longer be sovereign.

A double standard is unavoidably at work in the life of a strong and flourishing state: Its citizens observe limits in their conduct with each other, whereas for the state nothing is forbidden. If individuals in the pursuit of their private aims were to consider themselves as free of limits as Machiavelli's Prince in his conduct of the state, nothing being absolutely forbidden, then the actions of these individuals would immediately reduce society to chaos. The state would have become a mob; the Prince would have nothing to rule.

People have always believed—have seemed driven and determined, in the face of overwhelming countervailing evidence, to believe—that moral society as well as moral individual life is possible; that however rare or partial its actual achievement, it is in principle possible for individuals to live morally with the advantages of security, order, and opportunity provided by a powerful state, and for that state itself to behave morally with its constituents and with its neighbors. It was the accomplishment of Machiavelli, in a kind of Gödel's Proof of political economy, to show that such is not the case, that the good and moral life within an orderly society is contingent on the amorality of the state that makes it possible.

VII
—

Tarzan

AT NINE I passionately wanted a certain type of scooter. Two wheels in back, one in front, a platform to stand on that tilted forward and back with the shift of one's weight, this movement being translated by gears into the rotation of rear wheels. We were very poor, my mother and sister and I living on eighty dollars a month; and this scooter, my mother told me, was beyond our means. But I would not give up. I begged, I pleaded, I suggested that we could do without certain other things presumed to be necessities, I made budgets. We didn't have to get it right now, I said; it could be for Christmas. She was going to spend *something* for Christmas anyway. "Please, Mama, don't say no, say at least maybe." So finally, to get some peace, she said, "Well, maybe . . ." and of course, that meant yes. So then I pestered her to buy it soon, buy it now, "please, Mama, because if you wait till December, they will all be sold." But she does not have the money now. But she could make a deposit, I tell her. Just so they'll hold it. And again, finally, she says, "Well, maybe," which means yes.

But now I wonder: Has she actually done it? She tends to procrastinate. Maybe she's putting it off. So I start in on her about that. Has she actually, *really,* made the deposit? "I can't say," she says; "it's supposed to be for Christmas—isn't it?—*if* you get it. It's supposed to be a *surprise.*" But I want to *know.* I want to be sure. "You don't have to *tell* me," I say to her; "you don't have to say *anything* in words. I'll just ask you, 'Have you already got it?' and *if* you've got it, just move your eyelids a little bit."

She looks at me wonderingly. She is sitting on the back steps of our little house, I standing before her, bare feet in the still-warm earth. Dusk. Around us the empty flatness of Texas. The pink glow of sunset beginning to go purple. She leans forward, elbows on her knees. A pretty woman, still young, alone, poor, insecure, two children . . . and I before her twisting her fingers. *"Please,* Mama!" She gazes at me, her hands inert in my entreating and manipulative grasp. She looks away at the darkening horizon. I wait. And then, slowly, her eyelids flicker.

My father was a despot who rendered me powerless. But with his death I assumed absolute power over my mother.

AT ELEVEN I discover chess. Mr. Allison, a deacon of the church, shows me the moves. I am enthralled. Dazzling possibilities beckon. There before me, on that board, the most ruthless power, with murder in view, may be pursued, lawfully, permissibly, through patterns of great beauty, of intricate intellectuality. An immaculate sublimation, a red carpet for warded-off aggression. I ransack the chess shelf in the public library, study openings, mid-games, end games, begin to go for a Morphy-style, open game of reckless, slashing advance; and if, by profligate sacrifice, I can bring it about that only on my last breath, with my last ounce of strength, do I drive a dagger through the heart of the enemy king, then so much more grand the victory.

A few weeks later, in the evening, I am again in Mr. Allison's home, facing him over a board. Mrs. Allison sits nearby, knitting, rocking gently in her chair. Their children are grown and married; the two of them live alone in a small house at the end of a dirt road. He is a carpenter, a devout man; she teaches Sunday school. I move rapidly. Mr. Allison, shaken by my precocious mastery, takes his time, proceeds warily. Two hours go by. I feel the need to urinate. Gradually I am closing in, forcing him into a losing position. I advance a rook to the seventh rank. The pressure on his castled king is mounting, as is also the pressure in my bladder. Where is the bathroom? I look about surreptitiously. A tiny house, flimsy walls. They would hear the stream. Mrs. Allison knits calmly. The room is deathly silent. Mr. Allison moves a rook to the open queen's rook's file. His attack is coming too late, I've already got my teeth in his throat. An exchange of bishops enables me to put a knight on king knight 5. I squirm on the plush couch, rock slowly, front to back, side to side. Mrs. Allison rocks placidly in her chair. Why don't I ask? The overwhelming humiliation of the question . . . the intrusion of bodily need . . . I can't. I writhe. Why doesn't he move? Why doesn't he resign? Can't he *see* it's hopeless? Why don't *I* resign? . . . But with a sure win . . . it's crazy, would be perverse. If I should ask to use the bathroom, they would *hear*. Mr. Allison ponders patiently. I make little hopping movements. It shakes the table. He adjusts the pieces. The pain is unbearable.

Then it happens. Exploding. Suddenly, copiously, irresistibly flowing, silently, down my leg, into my shoe, onto the floor. With slow inevitability the smell of warm urine and wet wool rises between us. Mr. Allison shifts slightly, but—God rest his soul!—says not a word, registers the mishap only by taking somewhat less time with his next several moves and soon resigning.

I disappear into the night, in my wet pants and squishy shoe, know that I can never enter that house again.

A SPLENDID FELLOW, Peter, chunky, good-natured, quick-tempered, smart, a bit on the coarse side, fond of anal jokes. A strong player, he crouches in his chair as if to spring, sinks into the board; his face darkens; he growls. I lean back, away from the board, relaxed, move delicately, taking a piece between middle and ring fingers, palm up, lifting it lightly, putting it down like a feather. The more devastating the consequence of a move, the more important to me that it be executed lightly, elegantly. Peter grabs a piece in his fist, bangs it down.

One evening he is relentless, parrying every thrust, crowding me, driving me irresistibly toward impotence. Finally, after a long deliberation, he finds the crushing combination, crashes his bishop down on R6 as if driving a nail, jumps up out of his chair, tweaks my nose, roars, "Ho! Ho! Ho! Now I've gotcha!" and dances a little jig.

I am offended by this eruption of aggression, however jovial, into a game designed in its essence for the translation of such aggression into formal patterns. My nose tingles. I withdraw stiffly. Our weekly games come to an end.

"You're being stuffy," my wife says.

ALWAYS I delay calling my mother—because it is so hard to get off the phone. One thing reminds her of another; the chain of reminiscence is endless, not only ranges over her own long life, but gathers in friends and relatives, extends back into what her grandmother told her about her great-great-grandmother. After five or ten minutes I begin trying to say good-bye: "It's time for me to stop. I must help with dinner now." Whereupon she tells me what she has had for dinner, and the wonderful dinners her mother used to prepare, the vegetable garden when she was a child, and Mamie, the black cook, and the time when her sister Mittie Mae left the arsenic in the pantry and everybody got sick and they all thought it was Lit, the handyman, who had done it. "Now I really have to stop, Mother," I say; "there are things I have to do before—" "Yes, I know," she says, "and I mustn't keep you, but before we say good-bye, I want to tell you that . . ." and off into another story.

That's the way it was until her ninety-seventh year, when, one day, I realized with surprise that I had called her during my ten-minute break between patients, that I had fallen into the habit of calling at such times, and that it was easy to get off the phone. The stickiness was gone. Her densely peopled past had, like old film, faded to uniform gray.

When I go to visit her in the nursing home, I try to bring it back. "Do you remember our house in San Antonio?" She looks puzzled, then troubled. "No . . . I can't say I do. . . . Not exactly, no." I then describe it for her, the kitchen, the long veranda, the hackberry tree, the mesquite, the honeysuckle that covered the fence, the cot on the back porch where I slept. As I talk, I see in her face glimmers of recognition. I step up my pace, try to compact those glimmers into a chain reaction of recall. Everything is lost. I ask about her marriage. Nothing. Her years in college? Nothing. I remind her of the time when her father took her as a little girl on a riverboat to New Orleans, where, having bought an entire bunch of bananas, he locked her in the hotel room so she would be safe while he went off to play poker. The high point of her childhood. I've heard it a hundred times. Don't you remember? Nothing. She peers back into a void.

YOUNG BLACK WOMEN, enormous, slow-moving, strong, lift her off the bed into the wheelchair, onto the toilet, wipe her behind, bathe her, dry her, hold her up, dress her. She watches, helpless, troubled, as they ransack her drawers; things once carefully folded tumble about under heedless, uncaring hands as they search for underwear, nightgowns, hairbrush, dentures, blouses. She does not trust these women. She hides the candy I bring her in bottom drawers, inside vases, behind photographs.

She has misplaced her pearls. I search her handbags, her desk, her closet. Going through the pockets of her clothes, I come upon a piece of dry cake wrapped in Kleenex, half an apple, gray with age. Under a pile of stockings I find a carefully wrapped sandwich. "That's for the little boy," she says. But no pearls.

AS SHE LOST the past, she lost also the present. Vision blurred and dimmed; she could not read or write, could not make out what was happening on the television screen. Books and newspapers fell away. She no longer hears the telephone; I must call the nurses' station, ask that someone go to her room and pick it up for her. No more does she shuffle down the hallway in a walker; she lives in a wheelchair.

Emptied of past, bereft of present, without future, she begins to create an imaginary world. "The little boy has been hanging around today," she says; "I think he wants to talk to me, but he won't come close. I'm gonna get some candy; he'll like that." Over the months this little boy becomes a companion, a fixture in her life. She worries about him. Where are his parents? They should be looking after him. A little boy like that needs a home. He should not be out alone at night. She would take him in herself if she could, but it's hard for her to get about. Always she tries to feed him. In the dining room she asks the waitress to set a place for him. "Ain't no little boy here, Miz Wheelis," the waitress says. Whereupon my mother becomes cross, demands an additional plate, and, not getting it, puts aside some of her own food and takes it back to her room.

SHE LOOKS at her hands. Ancient, withered, discolored, gnarled with arthritis, leaping veins and tendons. A plain wedding band on her fourth finger, a large amethyst in gold setting on her middle finger. She touches them, hesitates, moves them back and forth, finally takes them off. "Look at them," she says. Her manner is portentous. Inside the wedding band: "OMT and ABW, June 19, 1908." "I want you to take them with you . . . to keep them safe." I protest: She enjoys them; she should keep them. "No. I'll lose them. You take care of them for me. Keep them safe. I want Joan to have them . . . someday." I drop them in my pocket. Her eyes follow their disappearance, linger on the pocket.

TIED TO their wheelchairs like rag dolls, sticklike shanks and arms, arthritic joints, backs twisted and humped, spindly necks, palsied hands and heads, vacant stares; some with napkins around their necks being fed by young black women, "C'mon, honey . . . open your

mouth . . . swallow it down . . . there's a good girl,"
food dribbling from their chins; some feeding themselves, dropping soup down their blouses, chasing peas
blindly around their plates with tremulous hands; some
slumped forward, heads on knees, oblivious of food, of
everything. Over the Muzak a muted rock and roll. The
young serving women talk of dates and dresses as they
shove food at withered, resisting mouths. A woman with
fixed stare croaks, "Silent night . . . holy night . . . all
is calm . . . all is bright." Another pounds the table in
a slow, insistent rhythm, chanting, "Tah!-rah!-rah!-
boom!-by!-yay!" My mother, hearing nearly gone, hears
this, lifts a finger: "The little boy is singing. He is singing your name." A woman with white hair flying wildly
recites in a child's falsetto:

Jesus loves me, this I know,
For the Bible tells me so.
Little ones to Him belong;
We are weak but He is strong.

On my next visit, as we sit talking, she seems to be
waiting for something. "Where are my rings?" she says.
"In San Francisco, Mother. Don't you remember? You
wanted me to look after them for you . . . so they
wouldn't get lost." "Yes . . . but I could wear them
while you're here. They'd be safe as long as you're with
me." "Well, that's true," I say, "and I'm sorry I didn't
think of it myself. Next time I'll bring them."
  A few months later I'm back, and give her the rings.
She receives them eagerly, hungrily; with something like

a sigh, a visible relaxation, she slips them on her fingers, she is whole again. During the next two days I watch her affirm herself in these rings. They contain the past that is lost to her. When it is time for me to go, she again, reluctantly, surrenders them. "No, Mother, I'm not going to take them. They would simply lie in my desk. Useless. But you really enjoy them. I want you to have them. I want you to wear them all the time."

THE VISIT is over. "Good-bye, Mama."

She fixes me with a look of solemn entreaty, "Son . . ." takes my hand, presses it between both her own, "Son . . . why don't you take me back with you? . . . I wouldn't be much trouble and I could help with the chores."

I look at the sagging eyelids, the clouded, unseeing eyes. Incontinent, diapered, having to be lifted onto the toilet, into bed, unable to feed herself, strapped in the chair that she not pitch forward. "I'd like to, Mama . . . but you're too weak to make the trip. You have to get back some strength first. Then I'll take you."

She looks at me dubiously, takes a grain of hope, but not more. It flickers briefly and fades. She stares at the wall, then turns to me in desperate resolve. "Well, I can tell you one thing," she says emphatically, "if you ever get down bad sick and have to be hospitalized . . . then I'm gonna come out there and look after you. I'm gonna come . . . even if I have to walk every step of the way. I'm gonna see to it that you get the *proper* medical care, and the *proper* food to help you get strong . . . and then I'm gonna stay a while."

ONE DAY, having neglected her for a while, I call the nurse to get my mother on the line. There comes the thin, vacant voice, changing to warm as she recognizes me. She wants to talk but has nothing to say. I chat, I tell her news of my children. She doesn't remember them. I describe them to her, relate her experiences with them, try to make them come back. Nothing. She does not remember that I live in California or she in Texas, does not know what month it is, what year. She reproaches herself for having neglected her parents recently. I tell her that they have been dead for fifty years and that she was a great comfort to them in their last illnesses. She is reassured. And when am I coming to see her? She thinks I am just around the corner, cannot imagine me two thousand miles away.

"And how is the little boy?" I ask. "Oh, he's all right . . . I reckon." "Do you talk to him?" "Oh, yes, I talk to him." "And does he answer you?" "He shies away. Don't seem to want much to do with me." "What's his name?" I have never asked this before. "Why, his name is . . . Allen"—a slow wonderment spreads out in her voice—"Wheelis. . . ." A slight startle of breath, a double take. "Funny"—she hesitates—"he has the same name as you!" Silence. I wait. Will she discover significance here or only coincidence? The moment drags, passes. Nothing. My childhood is lost to her. "Sometimes I won't see him for quite a spell," she says, "but then one day I'll hear a bloodcurdling yell"—she chuckles—"and then I'll know he's around."

That cry leaps from a deep well, without context or connection. She has no idea what it means, or why she feels comfort rather than alarm. But I know. I remember that cry and the fantastic power it claimed.

At twelve I discovered Tarzan and fashioned an identity on the life of this dauntless and unvanquishable savage. I would live in the jungle as he did, would survive on but my own strength and ingenuity, would be protector of all the friendly animals and the terror of the evil ones. I took Tarzan as my middle name. The trees roundabout were carved with the letters *ATW*. I wanted to depart civilization at once but knew I was too young. I had to wait . . . to prepare myself. But how long? Until sixteen, I decided. Then I would be ready. But would my mother let me go? I must get her promise.

I held close the details, said only that I wanted to live in Africa. "But at sixteen? . . . No. You have to go to college." "Please, Mama." "We don't have to decide now," she suggested; "you're only twelve." "Please, Mama. It's terribly important to me. Promise." "I can't promise such a thing, son. It might not be right for you. Let's wait." "I can't wait, Mama. I have to know now. *Please!*" She is silent, troubled. "A lot can happen between now and then," I add deviously, encouraging her to believe that I will change my mind about wanting to do such a thing, that therefore she will never have to deliver on this promise, while knowing that I will hold her to it even though I, in bad faith, seduced her into making it. "Just say yes. Please, Mama!" She sighs. "All right, hon."

The way is clear, the fantasy unrolls. At sixteen I will hitchhike to Galveston, will get a job on a freighter. Eventually this freighter will touch at Casablanca, where I will jump ship, find work on a coastal steamer going south. At the mouth of the Congo I'll pick up a riverboat, go upstream, deep into the interior. The river narrows. One night I will silently let myself over the side into the dark water, swim to the shore, disappear into the trackless jungle.

I viewed the next four years as preparation. I must become strong, must acquire the basic skills of survival. I raced down the veranda, leapt to the mesquite tree, swung about on the branches. I practiced climbing with ropes, threw spears, made flint knives. And frequently, after mortal combat, I rehearsed that celebrated moment of epiphany: Placing my right foot on the body of vanquished foe, I threw back my head, beat upon my chest, and uttered the victory cry of the bull ape. I had never heard such a cry, nor was I, in Texas, likely to. Knowing only that on hearing it, all the "denizens of the jungle" trembled, I improvised the loudest, most prolonged and alarming cry I could imagine, then practiced to make it uniform, distinctive, and terrifying.

And one afternoon, lost in my reverie, forgetting that my mother was entertaining the ladies of the Bible Society, I placed my foot on the body of Numa, the lion, and uttered my cry. And the ladies leapt to their feet, teacups flying, faces blanched at the murder evidently taking place in the next room. But my mother was tranquil and reassuring. "Oh, that's all right," she said; "pay it no mind. That's just Allen . . . practicing."

A TELEPHONE CALL from the nursing home. "Your mother is crawling around on the floor. We can't think what's got into her. Never been like this before. We pick her up, tie her in her chair, but first chance she gets she'll slip right out, sorta slide down, and then there she'll be, crawling around again." I ask the nurse to put her on the phone. After a while I hear the struggle, the labored breathing. "Hello, Mother. How are you?" Pause, then the thin, infinitely tired voice. "I guess I'm all right, son." I ask about the crawling. She begins to cry. "I've lost my rings."

VIII
—

Morality

THE HURDY-GURDY plays, and around and around they go, the charioteer, the legionnaire, the cuirassier, up and down, sailing around, the president, the foreign minister, the chiefs of staff, varnished faces frozen in arrogance and disdain, the bombardier, the cavalry-man, the machine gunner, around and around, as the band plays on.

WHEN the oppressed take up arms and rebel, they do so in the name of principles which assert basic human rights and so constitute an insurgent morality which justifies the overthrow of the existing order. The existing order has a morality of its own, an establishment morality, which holds that the security and welfare of each individual are contingent on the state, that the state therefore is owed allegiance, that its laws must be obeyed, its leaders respected. It labels the leaders of the rebellion as traitors, criminals, fanatics, and will crush them if it can. As rebels confront government troops, so insurgent morality confronts establishment morality. If government troops prevail, the insurgent morality is discredited, disappears. If the rebels are victorious, the establishment morality is discredited, succeeded by the insurgent morality.

In the latter event the insurgent morality comes to be allied with power, becomes the new establishment morality, ancillary to the protection and safeguarding of power. In this new role it sanctifies power, reassures the now newly oppressed that their oppression is in the nature of things, perhaps ordained by divine will, that no protest is indicated but rather patience and cooperation, that all must make sacrifices, that the leaders act for the welfare of all, that laws must be obeyed.

Thus a morality which began as protest against power becomes the servant of power. The insurgent morality in its insurgency declared that power is corrupt and tends to corrupt everyone and everything allied to it; and when the revolution succeeds, it proves the truth of its indictment by corrupting first those exalted principles under the banners of which it rode to power, along with the warriors who bore them.

THE MERRY-GO-ROUND spins, and around and around they go, the missileman, the submariner, the minister of propaganda, up and down, around and around, while the band plays on.

THOSE PERSONS who arrive at the intermediate ranges of power have clean hands, white lace cuffs. They are doctors, jurists, writers, scientists, artists, editors, professors, poets. They delegate to others the bloodier, the more immediately cruel and exploitative aspects of power. Thereby they create a space around themselves in which can flourish the gentler sentiments: love, empathy, pity, even self-sacrifice. These gentler sentiments then gradually constitute a morality which condemns the unfettered will to power.

People of this sequestered moral group increasingly criticize those more distant agencies which execute the will of the state, thereby becoming estranged from the source of their security and their affluence. Power becomes alien to them. They see it as brutal, abhorrent. They say the state is immoral—which it is. Increasingly they use their influence to restrict the state in its exercise of power over its constituents and over other states.

Thus an enclave of the privileged, who have distanced themselves from the bloody hands to which they owe their privileged state, articulates a morality that would manacle those hands.

A powerful society can afford, may even support and defend, such an enclave of the morally fastidious. But if the message of this minority should persuade the whole, the whole would find itself in peril. For force, as John Keegan has remarked, provides the ultimate constraint whereby all settled societies protect themselves against the enemies of order within and without. Those with the knowledge and will to use it stand close to the center of any society's power structure; power holders who lack such will or knowledge will find themselves driven from that center. Mercenaries will fight alongside citizen soldiers; but if there *are* no citizen soldiers, if all citizens maintain clean hands and all dirty work is delegated to mercenaries, then not for long will mercenaries be content to fight for wages. Wielding the force, they will proceed to take the power. Force, like a heat-seeking missile, finds out those who lack the will to use it.

IX

Psychoanalysis

SO LONG as his cowardice is manifest, the coward is despised by all, especially by other cowards who hope thereby to conceal their likeness to him. Ignominy is annihilating; the more shrewd the coward, therefore, the more likely he is to achieve protective coloration.

In Austin, Texas, in the thirties I could hear from Europe the premonitory rattle of war, could anticipate its spread across the Atlantic. Able-bodied, without children, a failing artist, nothing to excuse me from the coming draft, I would be a front-liner. I could already feel the bayoneted rifle in my hands, my revulsion at using it, my fear of having it used against me.

Cowards need intelligence and foresight: I discovered in myself an interest in medicine. As Hitler moved into Poland, I moved into the College of Physicians and Surgeons of Columbia University. Cowards often manage to appear brave: On Saipan and Okinawa I was a battalion surgeon with the Marines, it seeming but by mere chance I had nothing directly to do with rifles and bayonets.

SEVERAL PEOPLE love me. Many think highly of me. Were you to ask, they would tell you of my kindness, intelligence, generosity, empathy. And offer little by way of qualification—other than that I am difficult to know.

Viewing myself, I see a different person, find no ground for love. Anxious, petty, self-centered, tormented, meanspirited, weak. Too bad. I would have it otherwise, would wish for the noble features others ascribe to me. But I know myself better than they, make reference to a range of thought and feeling, of motivation and behavior, unavailable to them. Even those closest to me can know but a fraction of what I know. I've really got the dirt on me.

And beyond what I know lies what I have not permitted myself to know, wherein things even more damaging are hidden.

Since I intend in this work the utmost honesty, the reader, if I am successful, cannot in the end think well of me. If he does, I will have failed.

Is this credible? Is not every book written in the hope of love? Could any writer knowingly undertake such candor as would call for rejection?

Well . . . stranger things have happened. And anyway there's no end to my deviousness. Perhaps I'm angling for some kind of meta-acceptance; perhaps I hope the style with which . . . Enough!

SELF-AWARENESS comes into being in the midst of struggles for power and is immediately put to use. One defends oneself or seeks advantage by misrepresenting oneself. One doesn't think about it; it happens instantly, automatically, inalienably. It is not possible to abstain. One cannot be oneself. To be human is to be false. Awareness is inseparable from misrepresentation. The soul of self-awareness is deception.

ONE MUST bend the world to fit one's needs or bend one's needs to fit the world. Unafraid, one moves for power and bends the world; afraid, one flinches at power and bends one's self. The peasant thinks the prince has a free ride; the prince thinks the peasant's life is easy.

The bending of self is renunciation. But needs die hard. We can renounce the having, but not the desiring. The hungry nose against the glass of the patisserie; the young man alone, alone, on the windy street, seeing, as the Mercedes takes the corner, the pretty girl fling herself across the driver and kiss him on the mouth. What can one do with that? It won't go away. One is stuck with it, bitten by it, one turns it over and over, endlessly, the worm of envy burrows deeper, and it comes presently to seem that this agony of heart is unique, that it has never happened this way before, that it should be rendered in words.

And here, very indirectly, the warded-off, the renounced, is allowed back into play, for—who knows?—the novel about to be begun may prove a masterpiece. One will be acclaimed, honored, sought after by beautiful women; and here, exactly at this imagined future moment, is invoked the love that in the present one has not the nerve to seek. In the present it is hidden, out there somewhere perhaps, but withheld; one would have to go knocking on doors; but in that illusory future it will be lavished. Thus the strategy of withdrawing from power and changing the self may subtly transform itself into the ambition to change the world, by way of literary accomplishment, to fit one's needs.

My own first effort was titled *Come Away*—from Yeats.

Come away, O human child!
To the waters and the wild
With a faery, hand in hand
For the world's more full of weeping than you
*   can understand.*

Too full, anyway, to notice me; my gift is declined. Twenty years later I am still at it, this time it is called *The Elusive Anguish;* but the longed-for fame proves more elusive than the anguish. Everything fails. I am in a cage with invisible bars. I keep trying but see no new way of trying, and so lose hope.

FAILURE TWISTS the head around, forces the gaze inward. One is no longer a fixed entity in conflict with the world, trying to extract gratifications; the conflict is within, leading to change. Failure, like fear, is heuristic, moves toward intelligence, creativity, insight. It moves me toward psychoanalysis.

THE NOON LECTURE. It is 1946, Topeka, Kansas, the Winter Veterans Administration Hospital. We wait, one hundred psychiatric residents, all young doctors just home from the war. Disillusioned with politics, with medicine, we want to live in the realm of psychodynamics.

Dr. Knight is three minutes late. The room falls silent as he enters. He is our most admired teacher; we accord him a hushed respect and attention.

He proceeds to the front of the room, takes papers from his briefcase and places them on the table, faces the class. A large man, powerful shoulders, gray hair, ruddy complexion, pale blue eyes. He starts to speak, pauses, straightens his tie, tightens the knot, adjusts the handkerchief in his coat pocket, straightens his notes on the table, starts to speak, pauses. Again he straightens his notes, this time seeming intent on having them exactly in the center, each side of the notepaper parallel with the corresponding side of the table. The class watches with curiosity, then astonishment. At the first tittering he cuts the scene, sits behind the table. "Tell me what you have observed and what you can infer from it."

Since the announced topic of his lecture is obsessive-compulsive mechanisms, this is easy; two or three hands go up immediately. The first speaker gives a description of the behavior in terms of measuring, balancing, making symmetrical. He is stuck at the surface, will never be an analyst. The next speaks of the ambivalence of obsessional states, unconscious hostility being opposed and balanced by a precisely equal counterforce. Another identifies the motivating impulse as anal, and says that this origin, at the source of all dirtiness, explains why the defense takes the form of excessive neatness. Dr. Knight listens without reaction, calls impassively on one person after another. Presently my friend Jeff Monroe begins to rock slightly in his chair, coughs, clears his throat, grins, shoots up his arm.

"The Menninger Clinic keeps you very busy," he says. "You've probably seen four patients this morning, had a couple of hallway conferences, a dozen phone calls, and no time to think about this lecture or even to open your mail. You finish with your last patient at eleven-fifty and have just ten minutes to get across town. You drive fast, feel tense, resentful. Walking down the hall, you look at your watch, know you are late . . . so there's no time now even to stop and pee . . . and we must seem to you like a nest of hungry birds, mouths gaping, waiting to be fed. And just then the obsessional routine occurs to you. 'Let *them* do some of the work for a change.' And we have. We've given a quarter of your lecture. You seem now to have caught your breath, to be rested, and perhaps ready to take over the rest."

There is general laughter; I scribble a note and pass it to Jeff: "Now he won't say anything!"

"Are there other comments?" Dr. Knight asks. When there is no response, he stands, moves to the lectern. "I had meant to say something about my behavior," he says, "but I guess it has been pretty well covered. So, let's proceed—"

"Please excuse this interruption," I say, without asking permission. Dr. Knight looks up disapprovingly. "My interpretation of your foreplay to this lecture had to wait until you began talking . . . because it included the prediction that you would not say anything about it." There is a moment of apprehensive silence. The pale blue eyes settle intently on me; he is trying to remember my name. "You meant for your obsessional routine to be discussed at the level of the lecture you are about to give—a model of the sort of thing you're going to talk about. And that's where most of the comments have been pitched. Jeff's remarks went below that level, took you by surprise. You were amused—impressed, too, for they were accurate—but also uncomfortable, and hence annoyed. He was undressing you in public. So why did you not put him down? Because . . . the heart of analysis is to look elsewhere—to be presented with experience which the patient means to be understood at one level, but to see the significant motivation to lie at quite another level, in an area the patient does not want you to notice. And that's exactly what Jeff did with you. And for a student to do that to a professor is impertinent; but since you had presented us with a bit of clinical behavior and asked for an interpretation, you inadvertently gave him license to do just that, and so could not pull rank and put him in his place. But still it irks you; it was an invasion—particularly that part about no time to pee. So how can you punish him? Why, by not replying. By denying him the satisfaction of your admission that he was right. That is to say, *by behaving exactly like a resistant patient* who reacts to a correct but discomfiting interpretation with a brief silence, then changes the subject.

"All this, of course, raises the question of how you will react now to these comments of mine—and I have some ideas about that, too, but won't tell you because the telling would enable you to react otherwise . . . to punish *me*!"

For a few moments there is a dreadful silence; then Dr. Knight smiles slightly, and a ripple of nervous laughter flutters across the room. "With your permission and indulgence, Dr. Monroe . . . and yours, Dr. Wheelis—and if the punishment does not seem too harsh—I would like to get on with my lecture; for whatever you may think to the contrary and however rushed I may have been, I do have something to say, even some notes."

WE WERE showing off, leaping through the reductive hoops of the new analytic game. We wanted to get in the institute. All of us in this room were going to be psychiatrists, but few would become analysts. We wanted to be noticed.

And I *was* noticed. Afterward, in the hallway, another resident said to me, "Boy, are you in trouble! Might as well pack your bags!" but that was envy. Everyone knew that I was in. The age of psychology was beginning, and I had just stepped on the bandwagon.

And so was able, presently, to ask Dr. Knight to read

my novel, that cross on which I had been hanging for years. After a few weeks he called me to his office. "I don't think you can correct what's wrong with this book," he said, "until you are analyzed." Whatever else he said is forgotten, but there it was, in that one sentence, the mysterious glittering promise: Effort is unavailing; the underlying psychic mechanism must be modified. Then, *then!* all will be possible.

THERE ARE the seekers, and there are those others. The seekers are hoping still to find it; someone powerful and wise will lead them to it. Those others, knowing that what they yearn for does not exist, strain to escape a wounded self.

Two kinds of longing ensue. In the first instance, one's pain construed as remediable, a river of longing flows out to the healer. Though it may clamor for closeness, such longing is contingent on distance; for the master capable of such healing must obviously exist at a higher level than one's self. Should a condition of mutuality come about, belief would be lost. One sits at his feet— for as long as it takes. Perhaps forever. Such longing is the stuff of psychoanalysis.

In the second instance, construing one's pain as incurable, one longs to escape the self. One seeks a beautiful face, falls sick with desire. Such longing is not content with distance, wants union, a flying together like magnets, arms outstretched, rushing together, clinching, fusing. Such longing is the stuff of despair.

X

The Performer

CONNED by my own inhibition. The sidewalk in front of the health food store. A bright, sunny day. A flushed man in a straw hat, chanting, "Stop the bomb! Stop the bomb!" hands me an antinuclear leaflet, holds out an oatmal box with slotted top. "We must stop nuclear war," he says. "Help us out. Even if only a dollar." Worthy cause. Cheerful man. I reach in my pocket for a dollar, start stuffing it into the box. At that moment three things happen simultaneously: (1) I see that I have taken a five-dollar bill by mistake; (2) he says, "Oh, God bless you, sir! You have *made* my day!"; (3) I realize he is a charlatan. My fingers still touch the bill, but the jubilation in his voice, perhaps in anticipation of the drink he will now buy, prevents me from withdrawing it. Having been identified by him as generous, I am ashamed to reveal myself as prudent. The transaction is over. He instantly closes up shop and hurries away.

NEUROSIS is inhibition and anxiety. And what is normality? The freedom to love and to work. So we say. But is there not something disingenuous about this jaunty loftiness? What are we hiding? Normality is the free pursuit of power—curbed, in deference to prevailing morality, only enough to keep up appearances and to stay out of trouble.

THE CHILD grabs for power in whatever ways spontaneously suggest themselves to him, and in so doing encounters disapproval, punishment, loss of love—so bringing it about that the mere inclination toward forbidden behaviors causes fear, counsels caution. Eventually the parental prohibitions, installed as conscience, are honored as duty, enforced by guilt, elevated as right and as good.

Morality is fear that has been transformed into conscience. The morality that is observed, as distinct from the morality that is but professed, measures the freedom that individuals voluntarily surrender to the collective. Such additional freedoms as they may surrender measure their fear.

THE WILL TO POWER impels the rush of life; morality and fear constitute the barrier; the outcome in behavior is a compromise.

If the barrier is massive, the deflection of drive may be so great that no trace of power will stain the goal in view. But however masked or attenuated or denied, hunger for power is the source—for the selfless, the anchorite, the martyr, and the saint, no less than for the man on horseback.

WE SAY we want freedom and justice, and so we do; but when the tyrant is overthrown and the palace ransacked, the triumphant leaders of the revolution proceed to consolidate that power which was, all along, the unavowed aim ulterior to freedom and justice. We say we want love, and surely we do; but we want it to flow toward us, both tribute to and enhancement of our power; we are not eager that it flow outward, away from us to others who might perhaps need it more than we. We say we seek beauty, and truly we do; but having achieved it, we want the applause to be long and loud, to become an ovation, to sweep like a flame across the world.

WE SICKEN OF POWER, would give it up, forsake it. We push it away, avert our faces. We try to locate the moving principle of life in love or spirit or service or sacrifice. But power is inalienable. Renounced, it turns out to have been not renounced but curtailed. One simply reaches a point in the pursuit of power at which fear or scruple calls a halt. And there, at that point, inhibited from further pursuit, holding fast to what one has, one arrives at an uneasy equilibrium, alert to depredations equally from those who have more and from those who have less.

Each of us, all of us, every moment of our lives, eating or trying not to be eaten, pursuing or fleeing, struggling to achieve power or dodging its hammerblows—or huddled uneasily at some halfway position.

LISTEN to the writer on the couch:

"I seek what is distinctive in myself. Not to be blinded by the patterns of the world, by what I find in other people, by what is presented everywhere as the way things are, what life is, what it means to be human. These things come at me from all sides with great thrust, but I want not to accept, want to find, rather, what is unique in my experience. And, having found it, to shape words for what has never been said before. Because . . . if there *is* nothing unique, then there is no 'I' at all; what I took to be singular is but a stock item.

"But that's not all. Having uttered the unique, I want every reader suddenly to find it in himself. 'Me too,' the world must chant in chorus; 'I could not have said it, and until *you* said it did not know it existed, but *since* you said it, and *because* you said it, I find it in my own heart and so confirm your truth.' My uniqueness must slip effortlessly into other minds and there clone itself, my singularity then appear in the experience of everyone, spring up everywhere, like April flowers. What I lived alone in hideous idiosyncrasy and pain will now be lived by all in acceptance and mutuality. I will have fathered the world; like God, will have created it in my own image.

"I create self, defiantly, from the winds of contingency, then claim universality by extending that contingency to the furthermost limits of the known world.

"I want to be noticed, recognized, seen. I am a performer, I want people to come to the show. The more the better. I want even the SRO sold out. I want to write a best seller. Want to be loved. A lot. By everybody. Want to be important, to be famous. Nothing is enough. I want to be immortal. Let other people die, as they keep on doing, while I go on forever."

A POPULAR WRITER has more power than an unpopular writer. The writer who doesn't care is lying; no one willingly accepts lesser power. It may be that as between a small, elite, and loyal following and a large, lowbrow, and faithless one, he would choose the former, believing (perhaps correctly) that in the long run it would confer a more lasting renown. But it's a hard choice, and what he really wants is both. He wants to write something like *Doctor Zhivago* that will be hailed as a masterpiece by Edmund Wilson and at the same time will be in everybody's hands—on streetcars, airplanes, park benches, embassies, hotel lobbies, Greyhound buses. He wants to be on the cover of *Time*— *and* to win the Nobel Prize.

THE WRITER is I. Why the fiction of patient on couch? One needs a mask. Why then take it off? Perhaps I have made another. Can one imagine an honesty so ruthless it needs no place to hide?

Revealing myself, I remain hidden. As the real self is

exposed, it becomes false, the now real self retreating in shadow. Honesty cannot know itself; aware of telling the truth, I lie. The pure heart, blind to its own purity, sees only outward; the reflective heart is devious. Unaware of weeping, I show you a moment of authentic grief; be quick, it's gone in a flash. As I feel the tears on my face, knowing how they may alter *your* reaction, grief is mediated, is being staged. "Say everything that comes to mind," the analyst says to the analysand; but the second association is a comment on the first, and the third watches the second, and the bottom of that barrel can never be scraped. Below the deepest uncovering one yet deeper is possible. Dirt is endless. Fur and feces and bones, and ever deeper, but no bedrock. Authenticity is fugitive in self-referential systems; awareness builds layer by layer while reality flees forward.

THE ACTOR ONSTAGE, costumed as a Renaissance king, before sets portraying places he has never been, speaking lines he did not write and does not mean, engaged in actions foreign to his nature and intention—thereby creating form which purports to be a true map of human experience. And then there is the actor's everyday life, the shabby hotel, the unmade bed, the pee-stained underwear, parking tickets on the mirror, telephone messages from Yvette, stewardess on the Memphis flight, the drunk-driving summons, the letter from his uncle about the loan; and all this, we assume, is reality, the other being theater.

But is not this everyday life, this drab reality, also

theater? Is not this apparent formlessness in fact a maze of forms? Do we not secrete form constantly, by our very nature, as a cow produces milk? Do we not paste forms on reality like posters announcing theatrical performances? Are we not here, too, on the street, in the hotel room, costumed to an alien taste, speaking lines we do not mean, engaged in acts of an other's design? And is not this map of everyday reality, however sordid and dusty the credentials by which alone it asserts authenticity, as foreign to an unknown and unknowable reality lying somewhere beyond as everyday reality is to that Renaissance action onstage? Does not our most recent poster announce a play that ended, after a brief run, last year?

ALWAYS we are of two minds about power. Because we are insecure, we need someone above us, more powerful than we, to whom we can turn for protection and guidance. So great is this need it shapes our perception: We see our wise men as wiser than they are, our kings as more kingly, our priests as more holy. Being themselves but human, and having the same needs as we, they too are driven to look upward, to find someone or something more powerful than they. So we have gods. We kneel, we pray to an Almighty.

At the same time we distrust all power, know that it may not protect but exploit, may use us for its own ends. So we are poised for rebellion. When the wind veers, we will turn upon our leaders, tear them apart. The bodies of Mussolini and his mistress, strung up by the heels, swing from the lampposts in Milan.

TO GAIN POWER is to gain respect; it is also—equally, inevitably—to be hated. He who is afraid to be hated is handicapped in his pursuit of power, for with each gain in power will come an increase in hatred. The greater the fear of this hatred, the greater the obstacle to the pursuit. One continues on a course of increasing power until fear calls a halt.

Prudence requires that our hatred of the powerful be hidden, while our respect is manifest, often ostentatious. As every king must know, however, the hatred, though invisible, is always present. Uneasy lies the head . . . etc.

NAKED POWER is quicksilver, lost in a flash—a bank robber on the run, hand on gun, shot down at the next corner. So power rushes to form, which endows power with legitimacy, defines the processes whereby it is acquired, exercised, delegated, transferred. Hiding behind form, power acquires stability. Form is a structure of power but claims legitimacy as a map of reality. Reality is flux, while power insists on the permanence of forms; so form falls ever more at variance with the reality it claims truthfully to reflect. Power clings to form even after form's claim to truth has become manifest travesty. The emperor has no clothes.

THE ANNUAL MEETING of the American Psychoanalytic Association. The Hyatt Regency Hotel, a large

public room, carpeted floor. Folding chairs with silver-
ish plastic frames, padded seats and backs of maroon
vinyl, about two hundred in number; they stand about
loosely, not having been rearranged after the morning
session. Massive glittering chandeliers of gilt and Lucite,
heavy curtains, no outside light. On one side of the
room a stage, a long table covered with green felt, six
chairs, each place equipped with a gooseneck microphone. One man sits there alone, reading a sheaf of
notes. To the left a rostrum where the speaker will stand.
A few minutes before two in the afternoon. Thirty or
forty men and a few women are scattered about, looking at their programs, waiting, chatting. The chairman
mounts the stage, sits at the center position behind the
table. People drift in, stand in groups of two or three.
Those who are alone watch them curiously.

Some analysts are more important than others. The
important ones are sought after. The less important ones
hover about, hesitant, not wanting to risk rebuff, yet
not wanting to miss the opportunity of a personal
exchange with an important analyst. Nervous glances.
Shall I get up to greet that one? Or perhaps, if I wait,
he will come greet me. Should I sit beside Dr. X? He
has just been appointed to the Board of Professional
Standards. We had a chat at the midwinter meeting, he
seemed friendly . . . but maybe he is holding the chair
beside him for someone else.

The speakers' table is now full. The chairman is tap-
ping on the microphone, clearing his throat. People are
standing about, talking. The chairman continues to tap
and to clear his throat; now he speaks over the din,

asking people to be seated. Gradually silence and order are established. Doors are closed—and immediately are pushed open by newcomers. The chairman introduces Dr. A, the main speaker. The title of his paper is "The Myth of Pre-Oedipality." We already know what it is about; the program contains a précis: Genital strivings toward the parent of the opposite sex are present from birth; these impulses enter into all aspects of the oral and anal stages; we have overlooked them because, until the age of three or four, their manifestations are subtle; by the use, however, of twenty-four-hour continuous neonatal observation, together with certain remarkable reconstructions in the analyses of three adult patients, the thesis is established. *No* part of psychosexual development is pre-Oedipal. Though, of course, we must remain open to further . . . etc., etc.

He starts off with remarks of strained extemporaneity, glances about the room, smiles, tells a joke, gets a smattering of laughter, puts on his glasses. He reads in an even tone without emphasis or inflection, occasionally gestures awkwardly with his right arm. His paper begins with a clinical anecdote which marked, he tells us, the beginning of his interest in this subject, proceeds to a review of the literature. People stop listening. He drones on.

How are we to understand this scene? Everything the speaker has said, and his manner of saying it, his mien of being a serious searcher after truth, announce and define his motivation: He became interested in this subject by chance, he began to listen to his patients in a different way, became convinced that something important in child development had been overlooked; his interest was whetted, he began a research project, his findings confirmed his conjecture; he believes that his discoveries have important clinical applications, may enable depth analysis to reach even deeper; though his investigations are ongoing, and make no claim to finality, they have already reached a point where he wants to "share" them with his colleagues because, he believes, we will find them useful in our work and because our critical comments and suggestions will be helpful to him in his own further inquiry.

This is the official version. Dr. A does not altogether believe it. But he wants it to be true, and he wants others to believe it and, by their belief, to help him to believe it, and so he sweats to make it true. His manner of serious and portentous "sharing" proclaims his conviction. He has delivered this paper twice before, and the more he reads it, the more he comes to believe the official version. If he continues, he will lose sight altogether of what really drove him.

For years he has come to these meetings, has sat in just such audiences, listened to just such papers. Always his attention would wander; he would rather be somewhere else. Perhaps I might go to the bar, he would think, have a drink, meet a pretty woman, take her to my room, order a bottle of champagne, screw her. But it's too early for a drink. And I wouldn't meet anyone anyway. Be serious. For a few minutes he would listen again to the speaker; again his attention would wander, he would look about. There's the chairman of the Education Committee, an empty seat beside him. Should

I join him? No. Too obvious. Pay attention. Be serious. I want to get ahead. This is my professional organization. If I'm ever to get anywhere, this is where it has to be done. The form of power in psychoanalysis is the theory of its golden secrets, the rites of its mysteries. By contributing to this form, one acquires power. He looks up at the speaker. I would like to be in his place, up there at the podium, looking down. I know as much as he, I'm as smart as he, I want to do the talking, have others listen to me. What can I do? What ideas might I develop?

Now, some years later, he has done the work, written the paper, is claiming the power. He stands and looks down on those who sit and look up. He talks, they listen. He puts forth, they receive.

But power is never secure. He feels uneasy, cannot tell how they are responding. They seem restless, some moving about; several people leave. They *invited* him to speak, they *offered* the power, they *want* him to do well. If he does, they will applaud, will feel enriched, will confirm him in his power, perhaps offer more. At the same time they want him to fail, to show himself a fool. Something in them will relax, be gratified, and power will be withdrawn.

And the four discussants who presently will comment on his paper—each of them wants to comment so brilliantly that Dr. A's paper will seem paltry in comparison, and his power then devolve on them. Each discussant wants, next year, to be the main speaker.

And all those faces in the audience—are they, in accordance with the official version, listening intently in order to learn something new that will enhance their clinical work? Or are they not rather, like Dr. A in past years, restless, bored, thinking of other things, wanting themselves to be in his position.

XI

———

Hierarchies

WHEN INDIVIDUALS come together to form a social entity, there must be a period during which the association is revocable; the individuals may find themselves subject to more constraint than they are willing to accept, and may opt out. This revocable period is the hinge of life or death for the social organism; for if the individuals disperse, the larger entity disappears. This larger entity, driven by its own will to power, will therefore do everything it can to end this period of revocability as quickly as possible; for so soon as the association achieves such specialization as to make it impossible for the parts to opt out and survive, at just that point the association becomes irrevocable, and the organism no longer in danger of perishing by virtue of the willed dispersion of its components.

Aggregates, therefore, always act to increase the dependence of member components. The aggregate wants to bring it about that when the aggregate itself is endangered, its component parts will have no choice but to remain loyal. My country right or wrong.

When the mountain men came down out of the Rockies in the last century and took up life in the village, there was a period in which, if community constraints proved too onerous, they could pack back into the mountains and resume their isolated and independent existences. The present-day citizen of Denver or Butte or Taos has lost this option, is no longer capable of wilderness survival, and is held, moreover, by ties to the union or the grange, by the American Legion or the Rotary Club, and by Social Security, whence will come his pension.

THE AGGREGATE is not satisfied, however, to have its component parts stick together only because they could not survive on their own. Such allegiance is halfhearted. ("We have a terrible president, the country is on a disastrous course, but I guess we have to rally behind him. We have no choice.") The aggregate wants to generate patriotic fervor, to bring it about that individuals lose sight of their separate lives, lose awareness of their ubiquitous conflict with the state, that their identification with the state expunge the purview of individual life with its joys and sorrows, its hopes, its ideals, and particularly its ability to criticize the state in terms of reason, of common sense, and of the discrepancy between the announced aims of the state and the actions the state is undertaking. The unison of *Sieg Heil*'s by the packed and disciplined masses at Nuremburg, that is what the state wants; or the faith of Nikolai Rostov, who in holy warlike exaltation charges forward alone, an embodiment of the Russian spirit, against the massed French forces at Austerlitz. Think not of what your country can do for you, said President Kennedy, but of what you can do for your country.

There is, therefore, a constant struggle between the individual and the state. For the state to gain power, individuals must lose power. The state would like to eat up *all* individual power, all independence, discretion, freedom, autonomy. The individual opposes this demand, insists that the state not take any more. In times of danger to the state, however, individuals can be persuaded to relinquish additional bits of freedom, since the security of the individual rests ultimately with the security of the state. In a crisis we vote war credits and military conscription. And the state, knowing this, is always tempted to create crises that will justify arrogating additional increments of the independence of its components.

In this continuing struggle, our century has witnessed a decisive shift in favor of the state. The Fascist and Communist movements since 1917 have managed to appropriate vastly more power than citizens had ever in the past been willing to give up. The values of art, of individual conscience, of personal preference and belief, all presumably secure within the individual realm, have in our times been confiscated by the state.

Nor is this a vicissitude; it is a tendency. A tendency made almost invincible by modern technology, which, by virtue of its ever-increasing size, cost, complexity, and power, is, in this conflict, intrinsically on the side of the state. The nature of modern warfare and communication automatically empower the state at the expense of the individual.

Television exerts a steady pressure on the private person to live in the public world, in the ambience of the aggregate, with the values and the assumptions of the aggregate, rather than in the private sphere. Whatever is being shown on the screen, whether debates or advertising or talk shows, the viewer is always being instructed on how to live in the public world, while the private world is being subtly and insidiously impugned, is being made to disappear.

WE IN AMERICA like to think that our government is accountable. We are relieved when the president, though gaining power at an alarming rate, is reined in by Congress or the courts. But as we take comfort in the prudence of our constitutional checks and balances, we fail to note that nothing limits the action of the state as a whole. If the president and Congress concur in an action, then, though it be a monstrous crime, we will do it. At no time has this nation been willing to subject itself to the authority of a world court. We are willing to give an accounting of our actions in the United Nations, but if that body brands our account as lies— as at times it is—we will ignore the stricture and go our own way.

MORALITY CONSTRAINS individuals to serve the interests of power for the collective, in the way the behavior of cells and organs serves the interests of power for the organism. The man may be a killer, but he expects the parts of his body to be law-abiding. If one of his cells decides to follow its own lights, the man will correctly see this as a danger to the whole, will call it a "wild" cell, a cancer, and will destroy it if he can.

It has always been in the interest of power to conceal that morality is its handmaiden; we are trained by power to be blind to this subservience. The official version is as follows: *Morality is independent of power. It may be overcome by power but never usurped by power. The paradigm of morality is a man with a principle saying no to a man with a gun. It is always possible to say no to evil. That refusal is authorized by conscience, the voice of God within us. We know that some things must not be done. Every man is responsible, is accountable to his fellowman and to God.* We are justified, by these lights, in hanging men who did not say no. The Nazi warlords should have said no to Hitler. The sovereign state of Israel solemnly examined the evidence and decided that Eichmann should have said no.

The official version is a lie. The Nuremberg trials were public relations. The trials of Adolf Eichmann and of Lieutenant Calley were public relations. They were meant to demonstrate to the world that *our* states, the Western allies and Israel, are moral as sovereign entities. It is a lie: To be moral is to be subject to restraint; to be sovereign is to do as one sees fit. Israel is sovereign, does as it sees fit, and it does *not* want its high-level administrators to say no; it expects them, Eichmann-like, to implement policy. The United States does *not* want its ministers and generals to say no; once the course of action has been set, it expects them to follow through. We expect our lieutenants to do what their captains tell them to do. And we have any number of trained and loyal officers ready to perform as ordered when ordered to launch the missiles that will kill millions.

XII

—

The Individual and the State

THE COHESIVENESS of the group, achieved by morality and lawfulness, enables the group to become larger; and the larger the unified group, the greater its power. The morality of the individual thus has survival value for the amoral group and, insofar as the safety of the individual depends upon the power of the collective, also for the individual.

But the group can never govern itself, cannot, as a group, organize and exploit its potential power. For this, leaders are required, leaders with vision of how the group may become even stronger. And such leaders can appear only if certain individuals within the morally organized group are themselves immoral, break the rules in pursuit of personal power. So the greatest chance of survival falls, paradoxically, to that group which has achieved solidarity by morality and, at the same time, contains within itself a leaven of opportunists who will exploit that morality for personal power.

HE WHO WANTS POWER must be prepared to live flexibly between respecting rules and violating rules. Never must he break rules so flagrantly as to be flung out of the hierarchy; for the outcast will remain powerless. Since power can be gained only *within* the hierarchy, it is imperative that he remain in good standing with that part of the structure above him. Yet never must he observe the rules so respectfully as to miss the chance to seize unmerited advancement, to climb *over* someone above him on the ladder.

COMMITMENT to a cause conveys license to reach for power with a ruthlessness forbidden to purely personal interest. And the greater one's individual sacrifice in the service of that cause, the greater the license.

Hitler wept in shame and humiliation as Germany surrendered to the Allies in 1918. Darkness descended on him. "Only now did I realize," he wrote later, "how all personal suffering vanished in comparison with the misfortune of the Fatherland." He made a solemn vow: Should he regain his sight, he would consecrate his life to the resurrection of Germany. Voices summoned him. And then the miracle: He could see again. For what he proceeded thereafter to do he had the sanction of God.

FROM HORDE to clan to city to state, the progression is the function of a constant will to power acting on an accelerating progression of technological means. The spread of Christianity does not war with this will, but serves it; for Christianity supports the solidarity of the masses and thereby the increased power of the state.

State power contends with individual power. The hunger for power by the collective, with the aim of ruthless conquest, leads it to insist for the individual on a morality of self-sacrifice, on a willingness to die for the state, whereas the hunger for power in an individual leads him to ignore, insofar as he can do so safely, the morality required of him by the collective.

THE STATE exerts enormous power; the individual, even the very powerful individual, relatively little. It comes about, therefore, that those individuals who are gifted and able, and who in the pursuit of power are not much burdened by loyalty to shared beliefs, who indeed are skilled in professing and representing these beliefs while at the same time violating them in pursuit of personal aggrandizement, it comes about that these people strive for and achieve leadership and come thereby to be in the position of controlling and directing the enormous power of the state.

And just as the individual in his quest of personal power is likely not to announce his aim as such, perhaps not even to himself, but rather to advance it euphemistically ("I want to work with people"; "I am interested in research . . ."; "I seek a career in public service"), so those who determine the actions of the state likewise disguise the nature of those acts. They speak of securing national safety, of serving national interest, of supporting democracy in third world countries, of insuring civil rights, of preserving our democratic heritage; but under cover of these professed purposes the state acts to enlarge its power.

WHAT PREVENTS the achievement in reality of peaceful social arrangements is not chance, not accident, not fate, but the will to power of social aggregates. What makes for the inherent absurdity of great collective events, such as wars and revolutions, is that the will to power of nations, and the actions to which it leads them, and the consequences of these actions bear no relation to any reasonable goal of human conscience. So the individual of goodwill, with his ideals of peace, freedom, justice, equality—or even, more modestly, simple common sense—is confronted with something with which he cannot come to terms, an unfathomable and unyielding absurdity.

XIII
—

Instrumental Power and Charismatic Power

POWER IS PROTEAN. Physical strength, once of paramount importance as a source of power, has become insignificant. A slender man, these days, is not much disadvantaged. Not even a crippled man, like Roosevelt.

It is primarily in the relation of nation to nation that brute force is still the measure of power. When, during the Cuban missile crisis, the United States and Russia squared off against each other, the power of each was a function of bombs, ships, missiles, planes, tanks, armored divisions. These were the factors that each had to reckon with as it braced itself for struggle.

Power may be instrumental in nature—that is, directly related to one's ability to accomplish the work of the world. A good hunter has more power than a poor hunter because he brings back more game. A good teacher has more power than a poor teacher, an expert plumber than a novice, a skillful surgeon than a clumsy one.

Power may be charismatic, a function of one's ability to embody an archaic and unconscious representation of the primal father who protects against danger. At the time of the Cuban missile crisis, the power which each nation could deploy against the other was in the nature of firepower; but within each nation the enormous power, respectively, of Kennedy and of Khrushchev was charismatic, depending upon the ability of each to inspire belief that he individually did possess those magical powers which the peoples of those countries had as children experienced in their fathers and now unconsciously imputed to their leaders.

IN FEBRUARY 1942 Hitler stood at the podium in the Sportpalast and addressed ten thousand young men newly appointed lieutenants in the Wehrmacht and the Waffen SS. He told them truthfully of the disastrous reverses in Russia: Two hundred thousand German soldiers had already been killed, seven hundred thousand wounded, fifty thousand were missing, one hundred thousand disabled with frostbite. He told them it was their great and holy mission to save Germany and Western civilization from the Communist hordes.

The young officers were sitting in that vast hall looking up at the author of the war in which millions of their countrymen had already perished, and this man was now sending them east, where most of them would fall in mud and blood. Yet his speech moved them

deeply, aroused a profound patriotic passion. Many
began to weep. He evoked and shaped in them a mood
of fervent devotion and self-sacrifice. As they listened,
more and more they *wanted* to go. It would be a great
honor to die for such a leader. He who had created the
danger that now so gravely threatened them was able
to present himself convincingly as the Father who would
always protect them even as he dispatched them to their
deaths.

The new lieutenants had been ordered not to applaud,
but when Hitler started down the aisle, they could not
restrain themselves. They cheered wildly, many of them
leaping onto their chairs the better to see him.

MOST SIGNIFICANT POWER is composite, being both
instrumental and charismatic. The smaller the extent
of the power, the more likely it is to be instrumental.
A bookkeeper who has a good reputation and thereby
some power is likely to have it on the basis of actually
being an expert bookkeeper. The greater the power,
the more likely it is to be charismatic. A Hitler, a Chur-
chill, a Napoleon is likely to hold power primarily by
virtue of his ability symbolically to embody protection
from our deepest fears and gratification of our primi-
tive and grandiose fantasies, and perhaps not at all by
virtue of competence at directing the affairs of a nation.
Indeed, some such leaders, far from being competent
to govern, lead the nations for which they are responsible straight to destruction.

In between such extremes lies the middle range—

lawyers, doctors, corporation executives, university professors, foundation presidents, business consultants—where power is a composite of instrumental and charismatic elements. A surgeon of high repute and hence of power is likely to have a good deal of instrumental competence along with the ability, deriving from stately calm and silver hair, to inspire trust. A psychiatrist of high repute is more likely to have achieved that position largely by charismatic proficiency with but a modest component of instrumental skill. An eminent holy man is unlikely to have any instrumental competence at all. When a private becomes a corporal, the increment of added power is likely to mean that he has become a better soldier; but when a lieutenant general becomes a full general, no such inference is warranted.

INSTRUMENTAL POWER always precedes charismatic power. A boy watches his father at work, sees him build houses, observes that this ability yields power. He emulates his father, begins to assist him, gradually acquires his skills; eventually they work together. The pursuit of power may stop at this point; they are both skilled craftsmen, they command a certain respect, their power is instrumental. If, however, the young man's appetite for power is unimpeded, he will go further. He becomes a contractor, acquires authority *over* skilled craftsmen, begins himself to acquire different skills. He borrows money, buys land, becomes a developer, deals now with lawyers, real estate brokers, planning commissioners, city supervisors. He makes deals, becomes rich, runs for Congress, eventually becomes a senator. Now the power he wields is charismatic, has nothing to do with skill at the work he has been elected to carry forward.

THE CAVE DRAWINGS of Stone Age man bear witness to his preoccupying concern with animals as a source of food and as a source of danger. The ability to elude these animals, to capture or to kill them was the locus of power. Now anyone can shoot a rifle, no animal poses a threat, the ability to fell a charging elephant wins us no fame, perhaps even contempt, and we know that we may, if careless, destroy animals utterly.

Once nature was the danger and the challenge. Now anyone can use a chain saw or a tractor, and the moving of a mountain to make a freeway yields but slight power to the men who moved it.

All significant power now is power over people. The ability to win the respect, the belief, the support, the allegiance, the following, the obedience, of people— this is power.

MORALITY, law, and custom comprise the rules by which the group expects us to live. These rules allow for a modest accumulation of power by way of instrumental competence. If we respect the rules, we cannot hope for more. We shall be conformists, the salt of the earth but never its giants. This is a category of normality, officially extolled, but secretly despised: the herd animal, the prey of the used-car dealers.

A different order of normality, much admired by psychologists, calls for one to be as free in pursuit of power as a prudent, though often but nominal, regard for rules will permit. With less than that prudent regard, one is likely to land in disfavor or in jail—though sometimes, with a little luck, an adventurous thug may become a ruler. With more than a prudent regard one is handicapped in the race.

Neurotics are those who are crippled in the pursuit of power by internal constraints, impediments built into character by childhood experience. All of us start out weak in the hands of the strong, and a parent inclined to exploit that discrepancy can teach a child that any transgression of rules will yield pain and humiliation. Such an early education can bring it about that in later life, long after the tyrant is dead, any tentative reaching for power will be aborted by anxiety.

XIV

——

Fear

FEAR PROMPTS one to look about carefully, to take the measure of things. It leads to knowledge, is essential to good judgment. Without it one's vision of one's self and of the world is determined, not by the way things are but by one's will, one's desire. When power is absolute, distortion is extreme. The real world is replaced by fantasy.

In April 1942 Hitler, already possessed of greater power than any despot of the past, appeared before the Reichstag to ask for ultimate power: Every German was henceforth to follow his personal order or suffer death. The Reichstag deputies enthusiastically and unanimously approved the measure. He was now, legally, above any law.

So empowered, and thereby more and more out of touch with the reality he was imperiously undertaking to shape and to control, and with no compunction to heed the advice of his generals, who *were* in touch, he proceeded to make those disastrous mistakes which led to the destruction of the Sixth Army at Stalingrad and the loss of the war in the East.

NOTHING WITHIN impedes the pursuit of power by the state. Empires expand. Any one of them, were it able, would encompass the world. They go as far as they can, stop only where the lines of communication and supply are stretched too thin, where the conduits of power can no longer deliver effective force.

In the individual, however, morality is a brake and may at any point set a limit. A truly Christian position calls for the abnegation of power, requires one to give all he has to the poor, to be meek, to love his enemy, to turn the other cheek. A measure of the instinctual force of the drive for power is given by the rarity with which such an ethic has in fact been practiced.

Those Christians unable or unwilling to make so great a renunciation find much comfort in the doctrine of Adam Smith, who reasoned that the good of the group is best served by the selfishness of the individual, that buying cheap and selling dear serves God's inscrutable plan. The borrower being in dire need, the lender may righteously raise his usual rate of interest. The fame and influence of Adam Smith derive from his having reclaimed for the individual some of that will to power that Christian morality would have delivered to the collective.

The other internal obstacle is fear. One can go quite

far in the acquisition of instrumental power without struggling with another human being and hence without encountering fear; power grows as a function of skill in becoming a good pianist, carpenter, bookkeeper, or surgeon. But a point is reached eventually beyond which any further gain is achieved only in struggle with another person, in defeating or besting or outmaneuvering someone. In such contest one is vulnerable, there is no sure win. One may show one's self a fool, may be humiliated. Fear may become so intense that one's life comes to be structured around it. Whoever arranges for himself an isolated life (a writer, an artist, a forest-fire watcher, a drawbridge keeper) or a vocation with built-in advantages over the people with whom one deals (a psychoanalyst, an anesthesiologist) is likely to be one who feels keenly the danger of pursuing power through interpersonal struggle.

Often the danger, though intensely felt, is unreal. One cowers before a fantasy. Nothing bad would happen were one to move for power; but a wall of anxiety rises up, precludes the attempt. And sometimes, indeed, if one is persuaded that the danger is unreal, and thereupon acts in defiance of the anxiety, the anxiety itself—such is the creative power of neurosis—may actualize that humiliation which was expected to come from the outside: The knees may shake, the voice break, the persona shatter and collapse before an appalled and generally sympathetic audience.

THE COPLEY PLAZA HOTEL. A large room, several hundred people. Seven or eight men seated at a long table on the stage. One stands at a lectern in the center. A placard to one side identifies this gathering: Regional Psychoanalytic History: The Riggs Center, Stockbridge, Massachusetts, 1947–66. The panel members are all known to me. One by one they come to the lectern, relate their memories of the Riggs Center and of Robert P. Knight, its late director.

I came to Stockbridge with Bob Knight from Topeka in 1947. Came as a resident in training, stayed as a staff member. He was my teacher, my analyst, eventually my friend. I was with him shortly before he died. He meant a lot to me. As I listen, I am flooded with memories, with gratitude. I want to speak. I think of what I might say.

When I entered analysis, I was disappointed that I did not dream. For dreaming was, on Freud's authority, the royal road to the unconscious. You will begin to dream, Bob had said, when we work through your resistance. There must have been a lot of resistance, for I never did dream much. A few scraps and fragments to which I would associate diligently and which Bob would interpret, mostly images containing a pun, disclosing a rather simple comment from my unconscious. Once I was dismounting an enormous horse, sliding precariously from the saddle, fearing to break a leg. "Trying to get down off your high horse, eh?" Bob said. Another time I was falling victim to Mussolini, and Bob, claiming the role of dictator, reminded me that I had last seen him sitting at his desk, dictating. Such meanings never repelled me. I might well have dreamed them straight, was left puzzled by the need for disguise.

Later, when I entered training as an analyst, Bob supervised my first case. Some rules of thumb from that time are with me still. "Always remember," he said, "to consider the figures of a dream in three contexts: family, transference, and identity. Regardless of who they may appear to be, the figures of a dream are always mother, father, and siblings; they are, also, the patient in relation to his analyst; and, finally, they are always projected fragments of the patient's own identity."

He was a midwesterner, with that characteristic simplicity, straightforwardness, and decency of the flatlands. It always seemed strange to me and somehow touching that such a man should have gone in for the labyrinthine art of psychoanalysis—and should have been so good at it. He was a big man, six and a half feet tall with a large head and powerful arms and shoulders. At a case conference I could always tell when he was about to speak. He would lean forward, put his elbows on the table, the table would bend and creak, he would hunch those huge shoulders, look down at his hands, and begin putting into words—carefully, thoughtfully—an account of struggle, of conflict, of suffering, of an inferred structure of inner experience, so apt and convincing it could have been arrived at only by an unusual reach of empathy, those big hands opening up finally as if to release a butterfly.

A dark-haired woman beckoned, and he followed, leaving his family, at what cost in suffering or gain in happiness one can't know, but in any event not for long. Cancer, then surgery, radiation, and chemotherapy, followed by a remission during which I received from him a happy letter announcing his cure. Having spent his life discriminating between dream and reality, he was now himself living a dream, was dead within months.

The prepared talks are finished. The chairman invites comments from the floor. I raise my hand, am recognized, walk to a microphone in the center aisle. Am flooded with light. Suddenly my breathing has to be managed, my mouth is dry, weakness spreads through my limbs, my voice cracks, the prepared sentences fall in fragments. I hear a whimper in my voice. Everyone knows; it's a universal language. Shame sweeps over me. *Where* are those eloquent recollections? I grab desperately among the shards, stumble through a few abortive remarks, bow slightly, return to my seat. My heart is shaking my frame.

I am defeated, struck down by the anxiety that analysis was meant to relieve, at the very moment of paying tribute to the analyst who was supposed to direct that relief.

YET... there must be more than one way to meet the enemy. Even the enemy within. Don't give up. If you can't be brave, be grim. Be dogged.

AN ORDERLY holds the bridle. Marshal Ney stands beside his horse, looks through narrowed eyes across eight hundred yards of upsloping meadow to the massed Russian rifles, the artillery behind them, the movement of gunners, the cavalry in reserve. A mounted aide-de-camp ventures an observation: "Marshal, your knees are shaking." The marshal glances up briefly, puts his boot in the stirrup, swings to the saddle. "Let them shake," he says; "they would shake even more if they knew where I am going to take them."

X V

—

The Artist

ONE LIVES in constant conflict, largely unconscious, between the will to power and allegiance to shared beliefs. The relation is reciprocal: As the one increases, the other diminishes. If one is faithful to the received wisdom of his community, he restricts the drive for power to prescribed limits. He loses initiative but gains security, becomes a cell within an organism; nothing can then happen to him that does not happen to the community as a whole. But if he moves for power, he will violate the received wisdom, thereby losing the protection of the group. Corruption is the disposition to violate shared beliefs, and power can be achieved only by such violation.

The dangers of violating shared beliefs are learned in childhood. If the child is subject to severe discipline, he is likely to curtail his drive for power in exchange for safety within the group. If parents are tolerant of a child's willfulness, if he can break the rules without loss of love, then as an adult he is likely to pursue power with but nominal allegiance to the received wisdom.

POWER enlarges freedom; yet there is a way in which it also, and always insidiously, diminishes freedom. It webs one in expectations and obligations, commitments which must be met in order to maintain and augment that power—in order then to be able, with that greater power, to meet yet further expectations and to fulfill yet further obligations, in order to expand still further the ever-growing power. One cannot, so empowered, see the world with innocent eyes. One's eyes are in the service of a commanding interest; one sees the world in the way required by that interest.

THE ARTIST lives in the margin of terror. Faced with the incommensurability of his experience and the received wisdom, he is loyal to his experience. The received wisdom, he says, is not adequate, is not even true. The emperor has no clothes.

So art gives us courage to be ourselves—warts and walleyed and speaking in tongues. It sustains individualism and diversity, the right to difference. Those communities intent on suppressing difference, preventing change, and compelling loyalty to shared beliefs inevitably find themselves at odds with art. Authoritarian regimes silence artists.

A FAINT but terrible screaming pervades the world. In the plaza at the foot of Market Street, in the humid sunshine of Sunday afternoon, near the angular opulence of the Hyatt-Regency, craftsmen with their wares: potters, jewelers, sculptors, weavers, leatherworkers, photographers, artists; their works spread out so carefully on pads, or soiled sheets, or patches of black velour; no one buying; each little display a tiny universe, so easily kicked over or blown away or bundled up and put away in the trunk of a beaten-up old car in which the young man or woman will then sit and eat a stale cheese sandwich and drink a beer. And later, at home, I too, in my tiny universe: looking in the storeroom, in the dungeon, knowing I will never, ever be able to clean out this place, throw away what is of no use, it's too much, too heavy, someone else will have to do it, after I've gone, someone not so attached.

It fills all the space, blows over our faces, blows from the furthermost reaches of history, a fingernail scraping an endless blackboard.

I FEEL UNEASE. A vague disturbance, distraction. Something that might get worse, might become agitation. Something important I should be doing. It is Sunday. I am free. But am not free, not at ease, cannot enjoy the world. The feeling is not in my head exactly, or my heart, but somewhere near the middle. Deep inside. Perhaps the heart. A vague ache, a warning: something to be done. Before I die.

A postcard from Sulka. An advertisement. I sit at my

desk, look at the picture with a mournful longing that slowly becomes a pain, then drop the card in the waste-basket. Then retrieve it. The worm of envy gnaws deeper. A bed, a man lying on his side, shoulder raised, supporting himself on his left elbow, looking into the face of the young woman beside him. He is wearing a paisley silk dressing gown (that's what Sulka is trying to sell); she is in a nightgown, one breast partially exposed. Everything misty and poetic. His right arm lies across her chest. But he, *he,* can at any moment any time *he* wishes, move his hand upward, cup that breast in his fingers. He can also, *he,* if he wants, when-ever he wants, she won't resist, she loves him, will per-mit him anything—*he* can reach under her nightgown, slowly come up her thigh, into her pubic hair, into her crotch. That's when I feel the pain. He is very young, and very handsome. She is beautiful. Both have thick dark hair. Her pubic hair—I *know* it—is black, dense, a dark wood. A mournful panic sweeps over me. This way lies madness.

SILENTLY, irresistibly, we are moved backward. The crowd before us swells, stretches far ahead. The gen-eration behind us falls away. We are backed up to the edge.

"*I WAS IN PEET'S* this morning buying coffee . . . someone touched my arm. It was Peter Coyote." We are sitting in the kitchen having lunch. "We had a pleasant conversation. He's a very responsive guy . . . empathic . . . invites you in. . . . He likes Vicki's work very much. Thinks she's *really* a good writer. . . ."

The faintest of stinging in my eyes. But enough. My wife regards me curiously. Nothing escapes her. We eat in silence.

"And why are you so vulnerable?" she asks after a while.

"Why don't *you* tell *me?*"

"Oh . . ." She makes an impatient gesture. "You don't want to hear what I would say about that. . . . You had a terrible analysis. It didn't even touch your superego."

The light darkens. The purple plum outside the window bends under a sudden wind. Then stillness. I pour coffee.

"Well . . . I'll tell you," she says finally. "You're so guilty . . . all the time . . . that if anyone is even a little bit nice to you, it moves you to tears. . . . It wasn't even you, but your daughter. But that's close enough. Pouff! You're down on your knees in gratitude!"

I LOOK DOWN from the top floor of my tall house. Across the street a red Mercury convertible pulls up and stops. Top down. Two black men. They look up, survey my house top to bottom, side to side. Presently the driver notices me standing at the window. They drive on.

More and more robberies in this neighborhood. The police are overwhelmed. I worry, have trouble sleeping, imagine being waked at night by armed intruders.

I buy a gun, a Smith & Wesson .357 magnum. Force with which to oppose force; I will not be helpless. Whatever the form in which power is held and exercised, the ultimate expression of that power is force.

But there's a child in the house. Always the possibility of accident. I buy a metal cashbox, engage a cabinetmaker to construct a strong door for my bedside stand. During the day the ugly weapon lies locked in its metal box, the box locked in the cabinet. At bedtime both are opened. The loaded pistol is at hand. I am secure. Can stop any intruder, no matter how big he may be or how evil. Now I shall sleep.

But I can't. I find myself more wakeful than before. The fantasies continue, but with a difference. Now I am disturbed, not as the victim of force but as the possessor of force. Endless variations swarm through my mind. I imagine a knock on the bedroom door, a strange voice: "Open up!" Do I fire through the door? No. Unthinkable to kill without looking. I unlock the door, stand back quickly: "Halt! Hands up!" . . . And what if he does not halt? If he won't? I see a powerful man, unarmed, advancing. "Stop!" He's coming on, straight at me, a faint smile on his face. Do I shoot at his legs? And perhaps miss? And keep shooting? I have only six chances. Do I, at the last moment, when he stands directly before me, fire point-blank at his chest and kill him? One more instant of hesitation and he will reach out and take the gun away from me. I will then have armed my assailant and be worse off than had I faced him unarmed. Unlike me, *he* will be quite able to use it. The utter folly of pointing a gun one is unwilling to fire. Better kill him.

I run the scene through again. He's quite young, and stupid. And probably on drugs, to come at me that way. Shall I kill him? . . . I don't know, I don't know. . . . Don't try to decide now, I tell myself; wait till it happens. I may never happen.

But I can't leave it alone, can't be comfortable with that weapon beside me so long as I don't know what I would do with it. Night after night I play variations. After two weeks, exhausted, I reach a conclusion: I am unwilling to kill.

I dispose of the gun. Now I sleep again.

I am more afraid of using force than of having it used against me. What does this mean?

The gun is teeth for my aggression. The imagined exercise of this now lethal aggression prompts conscience to threaten a tidal wave of guilt. The balance tips; an assailant might spare me, whereas this guilt will surely destroy me. I remember Roy on that deserted road, a lifetime ago—the diverging paths, the path not taken.

Such abjuration of power at the behest of guilt may proceed so far that one becomes weightless, a wraith, may float away from earth altogether.

IN THE DEPARTMENT STORE. Overcoat collar turned up, scarf over my left shoulder, black hat low over my eyes, I wait. My wife is in the ladies' room. Christmas crowds flow around me. Swirl, eddy. I stand motionless against a pillar. Minutes pass.

I turn my head, catch a woman in the moment of her jaw going slack, her lips parting. Astonishment sweeps over her face. She veers toward me, arm outstretched, beginning to smile. She has a child in tow. "Oh, my God! I didn't think you were real! . . . Then you *moved!*" She laughs slightly, a dark, rich laugh, touches my arm. Through my jacket I feel her fingers. Again that slight laugh, relief and wonderment. Her large gray eyes make friendly contact: Though unexpected, I, refugee mannequin, am being welcomed to the realm of flesh. She nods, passes on.

Where is she? Where has she gone? I want to grab her, find her flesh under my fingers, feel it give, secure my reality in her yielding.

A FAST-MOVING TRAIN, teeming with people. A great din. All speak together, all struggle to be heard. The rocking motion throws us side to side. Rumble and clatter of wheels, groan and creak of metal. In some of the cars people are fighting, hurl each other out the doors, out the windows. More crowded now, more difficult to move. I am pushed backward, forced to the outside, am clinging on with fingertips. Cinders, the assaulting wind, the driving rain. Vision blurs, the landscape is featureless and dark. No lights, no homes, no roads. Fingers loosen. Music from within. A waltz. Ah . . . they're dancing.

I will leave this sweet monster soon. Rounding a curve, it will fling me away. Without slowing, it will hurtle on, rackety-rackety-rackety, clackety-clackety-clackety, without me, through the night.

Acknowledgments

THE AUTHOR acknowledges his indebtedness for passages concerning Hitler and Nazi Germany, to John Toland, *Adolf Hitler* (New York: Doubleday & Company, Inc., 1976); for comments about crowds and for the description of a Stone Age hunting pack, to Elias Canetti, *Crowds and Power* (New York: Continuum, 1978); for remarks about differences between male and female sexuality, to Donald Symons, *The Evolution of Human Sexuality* (New York: Oxford University Press, 1979). The statement of President McKinley is quoted by Reinhold Niebuhr, *Moral Man and Immoral Society* (New York: Charles Scribner's Sons, 1932).

The author is much indebted to Arlie and Adam Hochschild for careful critical readings, and is deeply grateful to Starling Lawrence for his initial belief in this work and for his patient, detailed criticism and support throughout several versions.